ANOTHER bundt® COLLECTION

BECAUSE YOU CAN NEVER
BAKE TOO MANY BUNDTS

BRIAN HART HOFFMAN

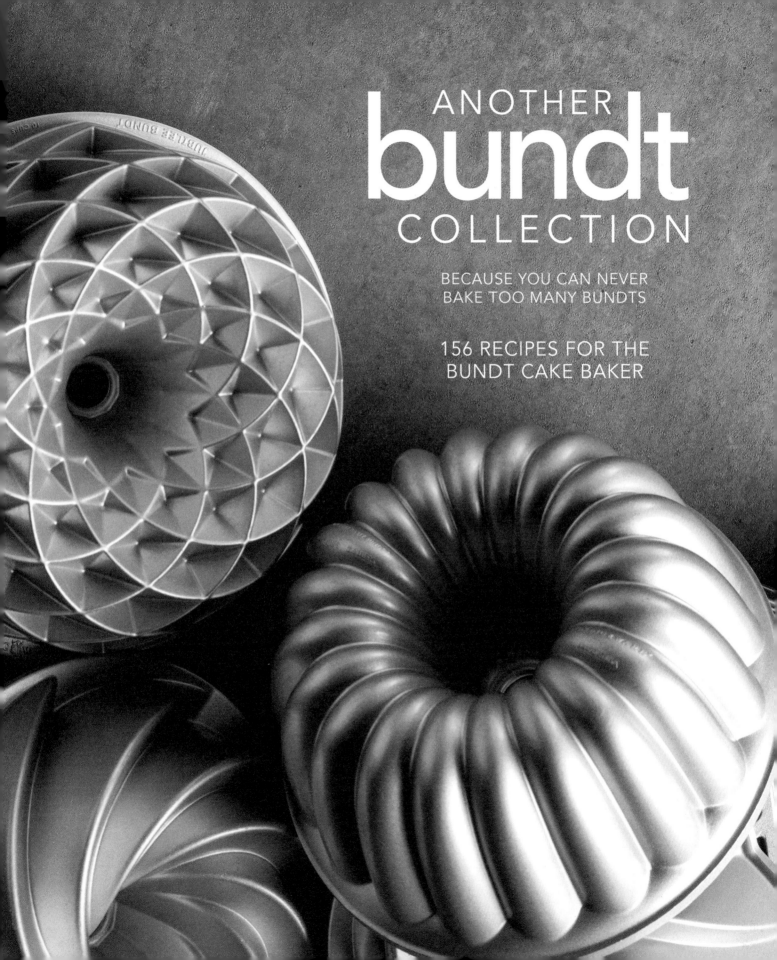

ANOTHER
bundt
COLLECTION

BECAUSE YOU CAN NEVER
BAKE TOO MANY BUNDTS

156 RECIPES FOR THE
BUNDT CAKE BAKER

83 Press
2323 2nd Avenue North
Birmingham, Alabama 35203
83press.com

ISBN: 978-0-9835984-6-6
Printed in China

contents

NOTHING
BUNDT
THE BEST

You've been asking for more Bundts, and the *Bake from Scratch* team and I are here for you! Through the years, I've heard countless stories of your deep-rooted adoration for the Bundt. So many of you, like me, have shared memories of a perfectly curved cake under a dome of glass, beckoning us to reach in and cut a slice.

Call it sleight of hand or trickery of equipment—the Bundt pan is an act of creative genius. What other kitchen tool can magically transform even the simplest batters into something that looks intricate and always impresses? It's all thanks to the Bundt pan. This iconic baking star inspired every creation in this book, which is chock-full of beautiful and delicious recipes we're sure you'll turn to for years to come. I'm also loving baking with Nordic Ware's Charlotte Cake Pan. I love how it instantly dresses up a one-layer cake and creates a perfectly flat surface for piling on whipped cream, frosting, fresh fruit, and anything else you want to add. Along with these tried-and-true creations, you'll find insightful methods, tips, tricks, and how-tos so you can bake the perfect Bundt time and again.

These pages delight in the breadth of the Bundt. In "Fresh & Fruity," vibrant flavors reign supreme with produce-filled cakes. "Just Because" is brimming with bakes, like my Butter Pecan Pound Cake, that make any day worthy of a celebration. "Chocolate Decadence" inspires and allures with indulgent Tunnel of Fudge Cake and more sinfully rich cocoa-filled creations. My "Spiced Just Right" collection highlights warm spices and sweet heat in Pumpkin Doughnut Cake and more. Rum, brandy, wine, and more spirits spike "Boozy Bakes," while peppermint, gingerbread, cranberry, ambrosia, and the like in "Holiday Classics" will fill you with festive cheer. And because we all need a little savory to balance the sweet, Everything Bagel Bundtwich Bread and more mouthwatering bakes are featured in "Savory & Yeasted."

Whether making its grand entrance at the end of a dinner party or made for no other reason than the pure pleasure of baking, a Bundt cake takes pride of place, inviting you, me, and everyone to share a slice or two and a smile.

POWER OF THE PAN

A LOOK AT THE MANY NORDIC WARE PANS USED IN THIS COOKBOOK

As long as the cup capacity of the pan matches the cup capacity called for in the recipe, you can bake our recipes in whichever Bundt pan you like

ANNIVERSARY BUNDT PAN
Capacity: 15 cups

CLASSIC CAST POUND CAKE AND **ANGEL FOOD PAN** Capacity: 18 cups

75TH ANNIVERSARY BRAIDED BUNDT PAN Capacity: 12 cups

ELEGANT PARTY BUNDT PAN
Capacity: 10 cups

SWIRL BUNDT PAN
Capacity: 10 cups

MAGNOLIA BUNDT PAN
Capacity: 10 cups

JUBILEE BUNDT PAN
Capacity: 10 cups

LET IT SNOW BUNDT PAN
Capacity: 10 cups

VERY MERRY BUNDT PAN
Capacity: 10 cups

STAR OF DAVID BUNDT PAN
Capacity: 10 cups

HERITAGE BUNDT PAN
Capacity: 10 cups

KUGELHOPF BUNDT PAN
Capacity: 10 cups

**70TH ANNIVERSARY
CROWN BUNDT PAN**
Capacity: 10 cups

PIROUETTE BUNDT PAN
Capacity: 10 cups

PUMPKIN PATCH BUNDT PAN
Capacity: 10 cups

CHARLOTTE CAKE PAN
Capacity: 6 cups

BUNDT PAN CONVERSION

IT'S EASY TO CONVERT A BREAD OR CAKE RECIPE TO BAKE AS A BUNDT, AS WELL AS TO CONVERT AN EXISTING BUNDT RECIPE TO BAKE IN A SMALLER OR LARGER BUNDT PAN

BUNDT TO BUNDT
USE SIMPLE MATH TO FIND A CONVERSION RATIO OF INGREDIENTS TO BAKE IN A SMALLER OR LARGER BUNDT PAN

First, get the volume of the pan you want to bake in. Next, get the volume of the original recipe. Now, divide the new volume by the original volume. This is your conversion ratio. Multiply all the original recipe's ingredient amounts by the conversion ratio. This works with weight (grams) and volume (cups) measurements, but weight is more exact. No matter which type of measure you use (weight or volume), be consistent throughout.

CONVERSION RATIO EXAMPLE

$$\frac{\text{NEW: } 10 \text{ cups}}{\text{ORIGINAL: } 6 \text{ cups}} = 1.67$$

ORIGINAL, 6 cups		NEW, 10 cups
6 ounces (170 grams) cream cheese	x 1.67 =	10 ounces (284 grams) cream cheese
¼ cup (57 grams) unsalted butter	x 1.67 =	6 tablespoons plus 2 teaspoons (95 grams) unsalted butter
2¾ cups (330 grams) confectioners' sugar	x 1.67 =	4½ cups plus 1½ tablespoons (551 grams) confectioners' sugar

A note about eggs: Use your best judgement when it comes to a converted recipe that uses less than a whole egg. If you are using weight (grams), you can beat the egg(s) and weigh the amount called for, but baked results will vary.

The conversion ratio also works to determine a new bake time. Using the example above, if the original bake time is 40 minutes, the new bake time will be about 65 minutes (40 x 1.67). However, pay attention to indicators of doneness more than actual bake time to ensure that your converted Bundt recipe does not over- or underbake.

ANOTHER PAN TO BUNDT
Begin by measuring the volume capacity of the Bundt pan you have. To do this, fill it two-thirds full with water and measure the amount of water. Now you have the cup capacity of the Bundt pan. Why only two-thirds full? To account for the rising batter or dough in the Bundt pan.

Next, measure the amount of batter your recipe makes. If the batter amount is approximately the same amount or less water that the Bundt pan holds when filled two-thirds full, your recipe is safe to bake in the Bundt.

PAN PREP

PREPPING THE PAN

Apply baking spray with flour just before adding batter to the pan. Spray lightly, holding the can about 8 inches away from the pan. Use a pastry brush to brush the spray gently and evenly up the sides and into the details of the pan, brushing away excess. Be sure to spray and brush the center funnel of the pan, too.

A NICE FIRM TAP

Firmly tap the pan several times on a countertop covered with a kitchen towel to help the batter settle into the crannies of the pan and release any air bubbles that may be trapped in the batter.

Look for this icon throughout the book for even more helpful information for specific recipes and Bundt pans.

TUNNEL AND SWIRL

If your recipe calls for a filling or a swirl, use our trench method. Add about half the batter to the pan (or whatever amount is specified in the recipe) and use the back of a spoon to create a shallow trench in the center of the batter. Then spoon or pipe the filling into the trench. If called for, gently swirl together the batter and the filling with a butter knife. Top with remaining batter.

LET IT COOL

Be sure to let your Bundt cool in the pan on a wire rack for the time specified in the recipe. This is essential to the cake removing cleanly and evenly from the pan. More or less time can cause the cake to stick to the pan and crack or break. To remove the cake from the pan, carefully invert it onto a wire rack, and let it cool completely or for the time indicated in the recipe.

FRESH & FRUITY

THESE BERRY- AND CITRUS-FILLED CAKES
ARE A DELIGHT ANY TIME OF DAY

BERRY SHORTCAKE BUNDT

Makes 1 (12-cup) Bundt cake

Gorgeously golden, our vanilla-scented cake is first divided into two layers before receiving a generous brushing of Orange Simple Syrup. Garnished with fresh berries after assembly, this Bundt replicates a giant strawberry shortcake, making it the perfect summer dessert to serve family and friends for any occasion!

¼   cup (56 grams) refined coconut oil, room temperature, plus more for brushing
1   cup (227 grams) unsalted butter, softened
2   cups (400 grams) granulated sugar
5   large eggs (250 grams), room temperature
1   teaspoon (6 grams) vanilla bean paste
2½   cups (313 grams) unbleached cake flour
1¾   teaspoons (3.5 grams) ground cardamom
1¼   teaspoons (3.75 grams) kosher salt
½   teaspoon (2.5 grams) baking soda
1   cup (240 grams) sour cream, room temperature
Orange Simple Syrup (recipe follows)
Vanilla Whipped Filling (recipe follows)
Mixed Berry Sauce (recipe follows)
Garnish: confectioners' sugar, fresh berries

1. Preheat oven to 325°F (170°C). Place a heatproof wire rack directly on oven rack, creating a sturdy, metal, crosshatched surface to help keep pan level.
2. In the bowl of a stand mixer, stir coconut oil by hand until smooth and softened. Add butter and granulated sugar; using the paddle attachment, beat at medium-low speed just until combined. Increase mixer speed to medium; beat until fluffy, 3 to 4 minutes, stopping to scrape sides of bowl. Add eggs, one at a time, beating well after each addition. Beat in vanilla bean paste. (Mixture may look a little broken, but batter will come together.)
3. In a medium bowl, whisk together flour, cardamom, salt, and baking soda. With mixer on low speed, gradually add flour mixture to butter mixture alternately with sour cream, beginning and ending with flour mixture, beating just until combined after each addition and stopping to scrape sides of bowl.
4. Using a pastry brush, brush a 12-cup Bundt pan evenly with coconut oil, spreading into an even layer; dust inside of pan with flour, shaking out excess. Spoon batter into prepared pan, smoothing top. Firmly tap pan on a kitchen towel-lined counter several times to settle batter and release any air bubbles.
5. Bake for 40 minutes. Rotate pan, and bake until a wooden pick inserted near center comes out clean and an instant-read thermometer inserted near center registers 200°F (93°C), 8 to 15 minutes more, loosely covering with foil during final 5 minutes of baking to prevent excess browning. Let cool in pan for 15 minutes. Using a small offset spatula, gently loosen center of cake. Invert cake onto a wire rack, and let cool completely. (See Notes.)
6. Level bottom of cooled cake, if desired. Place cake, cut side down, on a cutting board or a sheet of parchment paper. Using a serrated knife or a cake leveler, cut cake in half horizontally. (See Notes.) Carefully remove top half, and set aside. Transfer bottom half to a serving plate; brush Orange Simple Syrup on cut side of bottom half until mixture is used up. Spoon and spread Vanilla Whipped Filling onto bottom half; top with Mixed Berry Sauce. Place top half of cake, cut side down, on top of sauce, making sure to align design. Garnish with confectioners' sugar and berries, if desired.

Notes: *Refrigerating the cake while letting it cool completely can make the cake easier to level and handle when assembling.*

Pay attention to your pan's design when cutting your Bundt in half. You may want to slice a little off from center to ensure your top half stays intact when you need to move and stack it.

ORANGE SIMPLE SYRUP
Makes about ⅓ cup

3   tablespoons (36 grams) granulated sugar
3   tablespoons (45 grams) water
2   tablespoons (30 grams) orange liqueur*

1. In a small saucepan, heat sugar and 3 tablespoons (45 grams) water over medium heat, stirring frequently, until sugar dissolves. Remove from heat; stir in liqueur. Let cool completely before using.

*We used Grand Marnier. Fresh orange juice may be used instead, if desired, in the Orange Simple Syrup as well as in the Mixed Berry Sauce.

VANILLA WHIPPED FILLING
Makes about 2¾ cups

3   ounces (86 grams) cream cheese, softened
¼   cup (50 grams) granulated sugar
1   cup (240 grams) cold heavy whipping cream
1   teaspoon (6 grams) vanilla bean paste
⅛   teaspoon kosher salt

1. In the bowl of a stand mixer fitted with the whisk attachment, beat cream cheese and sugar at medium speed until smooth and well combined, about 1 minute, stopping to scrape sides of bowl. Reduce mixer speed to medium-low; gradually add one-third of cold cream, vanilla bean paste, and salt, beating until smooth and stopping to scrape sides of bowl. Gradually add remaining cold cream; increase mixer speed to medium, and beat until thickened and stiff peaks form. (Whip by hand toward end, if necessary, but do not overmix.) Use immediately.

Mixed Berry Sauce
Makes about 1½ cups

½   cup (100 grams) granulated sugar
1   tablespoon (8 grams) cornstarch
⅛   teaspoon kosher salt
⅓   cup (80 grams) water
1⅓   cups (200 grams) ¼-inch-thick sliced fresh strawberries
⅔   cup (130 grams) fresh raspberries
⅓   cup (63 grams) fresh blueberries
2   tablespoons (30 grams) orange liqueur

1. In a medium saucepan, whisk together sugar, cornstarch, and salt. Stir in ⅓ cup (80 grams) water until well combined; stir in half of strawberries and half of raspberries. Bring to a boil over medium heat, stirring frequently; cook until thickened, some berries have broken down, and an instant-read thermometer registers 200°F (93°C), about 4 minutes. Stir in blueberries, liqueur, remaining strawberries, and remaining raspberries. Remove from heat; transfer to a medium bowl, and let cool completely.

bake it a **BUNDT**LETTE

BERRY SHORTCAKE BUNDTLETTES

Makes 6 Bundtlettes

These miniature berry shortcakes are a refreshing summer treat filled with a bright Mixed Berry Sauce and a creamy Vanilla Whipped Filling. Cover with a sprinkle of confectioners' sugar and juicy, sweet berries for a stunning finish.

2   tablespoons (28 grams) refined coconut oil, room temperature, plus more for brushing
6   tablespoons (84 grams) unsalted butter, softened
¾   cup (150 grams) granulated sugar
2   large eggs (100 grams), room temperature
½   teaspoon (3 grams) vanilla bean paste
1   cup (125 grams) unbleached cake flour
¾   teaspoon (1.5 grams) ground cardamom
½   teaspoon (1.5 grams) kosher salt
¼   teaspoon (1.25 grams) baking soda
⅓   cup plus 1 tablespoon (95 grams) sour cream, room temperature
Orange Simple Syrup (recipe follows)
Vanilla Whipped Filling (recipe follows)
Mixed Berry Sauce (recipe follows)
Garnish: confectioners' sugar, fresh berries

1. Preheat oven to 325°F (170°C). Using a pastry brush, brush a 4- to 5-cup Bundtlette pan with coconut oil, spreading into an even layer; dust wells with flour, shaking out excess.
2. In the bowl of a stand mixer, stir coconut oil by hand until smooth and softened. Add butter and granulated sugar; using the paddle attachment, beat at medium-low speed just until combined. Increase mixer speed to medium, and beat until fluffy, 3 to 4 minutes, stopping to scrape sides of bowl. Add eggs, one at a time, beating well after each addition. Beat in vanilla bean paste. (Mixture may look a little broken, but batter will come together.)
3. In a medium bowl, whisk together flour, cardamom, salt, and baking soda. With mixer on low speed, gradually add flour mixture to butter mixture alternately with sour cream, beginning and ending with flour mixture, beating just until combined after each addition and stopping to scrape sides of bowl. Divide batter among prepared wells. Firmly tap pan on a kitchen towel-lined counter several times to settle batter and release any air bubbles.

4. Bake until a wooden pick inserted near center comes out clean, 13 to 18 minutes. Let cool in pan for 15 minutes. Invert cakes onto a wire rack, and let cool completely.
5. Using a serrated knife or a cake leveler, cut cooled cakes in half horizontally. Place bottom halves on a serving plate; brush Orange Simple Syrup on bottom halves of cakes until mixture is used up. Spoon and spread Vanilla Whipped Filling onto bottom halves of cakes; top with Mixed Berry Sauce. Place top halves of cakes, cut side down, on top of sauce, making sure to align designs. Garnish with confectioners' sugar and berries, if desired.

ORANGE SIMPLE SYRUP
Makes about ¼ cup

2   tablespoons (24 grams) granulated sugar
2   tablespoons (30 grams) water
4   teaspoons (20 grams) orange liqueur*

1. In a small microwave-safe bowl, stir together sugar and 2 tablespoons (30 grams) water. Heat on high in 10- to 20-second intervals, stirring between each, until sugar dissolves. Stir in liqueur. Let cool completely before using.

*We used Grand Marnier. Fresh orange juice may be used instead, if desired, in the Orange Simple Syrup as well as in the Mixed Berry Sauce.

VANILLA WHIPPED FILLING
Makes about 1½ cups

2   ounces (56 grams) cream cheese, softened
3   tablespoons (36 grams) granulated sugar
⅔   cup (160 grams) cold heavy whipping cream
½   teaspoon (3 grams) vanilla bean paste
⅛   teaspoon kosher salt

1. In the bowl of a stand mixer, whisk together cream cheese and sugar by hand until smooth and well combined. Using the whisk attachment, with mixer on medium-low speed, slowly add one-third of cold cream, vanilla bean paste, and salt, beating until smooth and stopping to scrape sides of bowl. Gradually add remaining cold cream; increase mixer speed to medium, and beat until thickened and stiff peaks form. (Whisk by hand toward end, if necessary, but do not overmix; see Note.) Use immediately.

Note: *If this amount is too small for your stand mixer, a hand mixer can be used instead.*

MIXED BERRY SAUCE
Makes about 1 cup

¼   cup (50 grams) granulated sugar
1½   teaspoons (4.5 grams) cornstarch
Pinch kosher salt
2½   tablespoons (37.5 grams) water

bake FROM SCRATCH™
BUNDTOLOGY

Coating the Nordic Ware 75th Anniversary Braided Bundt Pan with coconut oil and flour releases the cake cleanly with crisp edges and an elegant interwoven design.

Refrigerating this Bundt while letting it cool completely can make the cake easier to level and handle while assembling.

With its tighter crumb, this cake not only bakes beautifully but also boasts a sturdy structure for cutting in half and layering. Meanwhile, a mix of coconut oil, butter, and sour cream keeps every bite tasty, moist, and tender.

Assess the cake's design before cutting your Bundt in half. You may want to slice a little off-center to ensure your top half stays intact while moving and stacking.

A simple syrup spiked with orange liqueur adds an extra punch of moisture and flavor. For an alcohol-free option, swap in fresh orange juice for the liqueur in the syrup and in the Mixed Berry Sauce.

⅔ cup (100 grams) ¼-inch-thick sliced fresh strawberries
½ cup (85 grams) fresh raspberries
¼ cup (40 grams) fresh blueberries
1 tablespoon (15 grams) orange liqueur

1. In a medium saucepan, whisk together sugar, cornstarch, and salt. Stir in 2½ tablespoons (37.5 grams) water until well combined; stir in half of strawberries and half of raspberries. Bring to a boil over medium heat, stirring frequently; cook until thickened, some berries have broken down, and an instant-read thermometer registers 200°F (93°C), 2 to 4 minutes. (Keep an eye on berry mixture; timing may vary depending on stovetop.) Stir in blueberries, liqueur, remaining strawberries, and remaining raspberries. Remove from heat; transfer to a medium bowl, and let cool completely.

KEY LIME BUNDT CAKE

Makes 1 (15-cup) Bundt cake

We love Key limes, so it's no surprise that we are obsessed with this cake! It has an extra dose of lovely tang courtesy of buttermilk in the batter and glaze.

8 ounces (226 grams) cream cheese, softened
3 cups (375 grams) plus 2 tablespoons (16 grams) all-purpose flour, divided
⅓ cup (80 grams) plus 2 tablespoons (30 grams) Key lime juice (from bottle), divided
2 tablespoons (40 grams) sweetened condensed milk
5 large eggs (250 grams), room temperature and divided
1 cup (227 grams) unsalted butter, softened
1¾ cups (350 grams) granulated sugar, divided
½ cup (110 grams) firmly packed light brown sugar
3 tablespoons (9 grams) tightly packed lime zest (about 5 medium limes)
2 tablespoons (15 grams) finely ground graham cracker crumbs
1 teaspoon (3 grams) kosher salt
½ teaspoon (2.5 grams) baking soda
1¼ cups (300 grams) whole buttermilk, room temperature
Sweet Buttermilk Glaze (recipe follows)
Garnish: Key lime slices

1. Preheat oven to 325°F (170°C).
2. In the bowl of a stand mixer fitted with the paddle attachment, beat cream cheese, 2 tablespoons (16 grams) flour, 2 tablespoons (30 grams) lime juice, and condensed milk at medium speed until smooth and well combined, 1 to 2 minutes, stopping to scrape sides of bowl. Add 1 egg (50 grams); beat until well combined. Transfer mixture to a small bowl; refrigerate for 30 to 40 minutes.
3. Clean bowl of stand mixer and paddle. Using the paddle attachment, beat butter, 1½ cups (300 grams) granulated sugar, brown sugar, and lime zest at medium-low speed just until combined; increase mixer speed to medium, and beat until fluffy, 3 to 4 minutes, stopping to scrape sides of bowl. Add remaining 4 eggs (200 grams), one at a time, beating until well combined after each addition. (Mixture may look curdled at this point but will come together when flour is added.)

4. In a large bowl, whisk together graham cracker crumbs, salt, baking soda, and remaining 3 cups (375 grams) flour. With mixer on low speed, gradually add graham cracker mixture to butter mixture alternately with buttermilk, beginning and ending with graham cracker mixture, beating just until combined and stopping to scrape sides of bowl.
5. Spray a 15-cup Bundt pan with baking spray with flour. Spoon 3½ cups (865 grams) batter into prepared pan. Gently tap pan on a kitchen towel-lined counter several times to settle batter and release any air bubbles. Using an offset spatula, spread batter up sides and center of pan, creating a ½-inch-deep trench. Dollop cream cheese mixture over batter in trench, avoiding edges of pan. Drag a knife through center of each dollop to swirl into batter. Scoop remaining batter in small dollops on top of filling, and gently smooth, covering cream cheese mixture.
6. Bake until a wooden pick inserted near center comes out clean, 1 hour and 5 minutes to 1 hour and 15 minutes, loosely covering with foil to prevent excess browning, if necessary. Let cool in pan for 20 minutes.
7. In a small bowl, stir together remaining ⅓ cup (80 grams) lime juice and remaining ¼ cup (50 grams) granulated sugar.
8. Using a small offset spatula, gently loosen cake from center of pan. Invert cake onto a wire rack over a rimmed baking sheet. Gently brush juice mixture all over cake. Let cool completely.
9. Spoon and spread Sweet Buttermilk Glaze over cooled cake as desired. Garnish with lime slices, if desired. Cover and refrigerate for up to 3 days.

SWEET BUTTERMILK GLAZE
Makes about ½ cup

¾ cup (90 grams) confectioners' sugar
1¼ tablespoons (19 grams) whole buttermilk
1 tablespoon (14 grams) unsalted butter, melted
1½ teaspoons (10 grams) sweetened condensed milk

1. In a medium bowl, whisk together all ingredients until smooth and well combined. Use immediately.

TRIPLE-STRAWBERRY POUND CAKE

Makes 1 (10-inch) cake

Slice into this unassuming Triple-Strawberry Pound Cake to find a surprise berry-brilliant interior. In sweet shades of strawberry and vanilla ombré, this velvety Triple-Strawberry Pound Cake is the epitome of the colors and flavors of spring.

2	cups (454 grams) unsalted butter, softened
3	cups (600 grams) granulated sugar
1	teaspoon (3 grams) kosher salt
7	large eggs (350 grams), room temperature
2	teaspoons (8 grams) vanilla extract
3½	cups (438 grams) all-purpose flour, divided
⅓	cup (80 grams) sour cream
½	cup (160 grams) strawberry preserves, divided
16	drops red liquid food coloring*, divided
1½	cups (30 grams) freeze-dried strawberries

Strawberry Glaze (recipe follows)
Garnish: fresh strawberries

1. Preheat oven to 300°F (150°C). Butter and flour a 10-inch tube pan. Wrap exterior of pan in foil with shiny side facing out. (See Note.)
2. In the bowl of a stand mixer fitted with the paddle attachment, beat butter, sugar, and salt at medium speed until fluffy, 6 to 7 minutes, stopping to scrape sides of bowl. Add eggs, one at a time, beating well after each addition. Beat in vanilla. Divide batter among 3 bowls (460 grams each).
3. In first bowl, fold in 1¼ cups (156 grams) flour alternately with sour cream, beginning and ending with flour, just until combined. Set aside.
4. In second bowl, fold in 1 cup plus 2 tablespoons (141 grams) flour alternately with ¼ cup (80 grams) preserves and 6 drops food coloring, beginning and ending with flour, just until combined. Set aside.

5. In the container of a blender, blend freeze-dried strawberries to a fine powder.
6. In a small bowl, whisk together ¼ cup (21 grams) strawberry powder and remaining 1 cup plus 2 tablespoons (141 grams) flour. Fold flour mixture into remaining batter alternately with remaining ¼ cup (80 grams) preserves and remaining 10 drops food coloring, beginning and ending with flour mixture, just until combined.
7. Spoon plain vanilla batter into prepared pan, smoothing top. Gently spoon light pink batter on top, smoothing top. Gently spoon dark pink batter on top, smoothing top.
8. Bake until a wooden pick inserted near center comes out clean or an instant-read thermometer inserted near center registers 205°F (96°C) to 210°F (99°C), 2 hours to 2 hours and 10 minutes, loosely covering top of pan with foil after 1 hour and 15 minutes of baking to prevent excess browning. Let cool in pan for 15 minutes. Invert cake onto a plate, and unmold from pan. Let cool completely on a wire rack. Top with Strawberry Glaze. Garnish with strawberries, if desired.

*We used McCormick Red Food Color. You can also use gel food coloring, but the color will not be as vibrant.

Note: *Because this cake has a long bake time, we wrapped the pan in foil to prevent the crust from becoming too dark. The foil shield also helps the cake rise and bake evenly.*

STRAWBERRY GLAZE
Makes ¾ cup

1½	cups (180 grams) confectioners' sugar
¼	cup plus 2 tablespoons (120 grams) strawberry preserves
1½	teaspoons (7.5 grams) whole milk

1. In a medium bowl, whisk together all ingredients until smooth. Use immediately.

BANANA STREUSEL BREAD

Makes 1 (15-cup) loaf

Why yes, banana bread will Bundt. In this incarnation, our banana bread is an inverted Bundt beauty, boasting a crunchy cinnamon streusel topping that proves more addictive with each serving.

3¾ cups (469 grams) all-purpose flour, divided
1½ cups (330 grams) plus 2 tablespoons (28 grams) firmly packed light brown sugar, divided
1⅓ cups (267 grams) plus 2 tablespoons (24 grams) granulated sugar, divided
1¾ teaspoons (3.5 grams) ground cinnamon, divided
4 teaspoons (20 grams) unsalted butter, cubed
2 cups (476 grams) mashed ripe banana (about 6 medium bananas)
1 cup (214 grams) vegetable oil
⅔ cup (160 grams) sour cream, room temperature
4 large eggs (200 grams), room temperature
1 tablespoon (13 grams) vanilla extract
2 teaspoons (10 grams) baking powder
1¼ teaspoons (6.25 grams) baking soda
1¼ teaspoons (3.75 grams) kosher salt
½ teaspoon (1 gram) ground cloves
¼ teaspoon ground nutmeg

1. Preheat oven to 350°F (180°C).
2. In a medium bowl, stir together ¼ cup (31 grams) flour, 2 tablespoons (28 grams) brown sugar, 2 tablespoons (24 grams) granulated sugar, and ¾ teaspoon (1.5 grams) cinnamon. Add butter; using your fingers or 2 forks, work butter into flour mixture until mixture resembles coarse crumbs or slightly wet sand. Set aside.
3. In the bowl of a stand mixer fitted with the paddle attachment, beat banana, oil, sour cream, eggs, vanilla, remaining 1½ cups (330 grams) brown sugar, and remaining 1⅓ cups (267 grams) granulated sugar at medium-low speed until well combined, about 2 minutes, stopping to scrape sides of bowl.
4. In another medium bowl, whisk together baking powder, baking soda, salt, cloves, nutmeg, remaining 3½ cups (438 grams) flour, and remaining 1 teaspoon (2 grams) cinnamon. With mixer on low speed, gradually add baking powder mixture to banana mixture, beating until combined and stopping to scrape sides of bowl.
5. Spray a 15-cup Nordic Ware Anniversary Bundt Pan with baking spray with flour. Pour batter into prepared pan. Tap pan on a kitchen towel-lined counter a few times to settle batter and release any air bubbles.
6. Bake for 20 minutes. Sprinkle with streusel, and bake until golden brown and a wooden pick inserted near center comes out clean, 40 to 55 minutes more, rotating pan halfway through baking and loosely covering with foil to prevent excess browning, if necessary. Let cool in pan on a wire rack for 20 minutes.
7. Using a small offset spatula, loosen bread from center of pan. Slowly invert bread onto a wire rack placed over a rimmed baking sheet. (Some streusel will fall off.) Using a large, flat plate or a cake lifter, turn bread streusel side up, and place on wire rack; let cool completely.

ROASTED STRAWBERRY-MASCARPONE BUNDT CAKE

Makes 1 (10-cup) Bundt cake

We're letting you in on a big baking secret: roast your strawberries. We roasted 2 pounds of spring strawberries with a bit of sugar, concentrating their sweet flavor and creating a delicious strawberry syrup. We incorporated it into the glaze, creating a pretty-in-pink topping worthy of this epic cake.

2   pounds (907 grams) fresh strawberries (see Note) (halved or quartered if large)
1¾   cups (350 grams) plus 2 tablespoons (24 grams) granulated sugar, divided
1½   teaspoons (3.75 grams) kosher salt, divided
¾   cup (170 grams) unsalted butter, softened
3   large eggs (150 grams), room temperature
1   teaspoon (4 grams) vanilla extract
½   teaspoon (2 grams) almond extract
2½   cups (313 grams) all-purpose flour
1   tablespoon (15 grams) baking powder
⅔   cup (160 grams) mascarpone cheese, room temperature
¼   cup (60 grams) plus 1 tablespoon (15 grams) water, room temperature and divided
Roasted Strawberry Glaze (recipe follows)

1. Preheat oven to 375°F (190°C). Line a rimmed baking sheet with parchment paper.
2. In a 13x9-inch baking dish, stir together strawberries, ¼ cup (50 grams) sugar, and ¼ teaspoon salt until well combined.
3. Bake until berries are very soft, fragrant, and have released a lot of liquid, about 30 minutes, stirring every 10 minutes. Using a slotted spoon, transfer strawberries to prepared baking sheet. Reserve roasted strawberry juice in a 1-cup glass measuring cup or small bowl. Let strawberries cool to room temperature; chop into ¼-inch pieces. Reduce oven temperature to 325°F (163°C).
4. In the bowl of a stand mixer fitted with the paddle attachment, beat butter and 1½ cups (300 grams) sugar at medium-low speed until fluffy, 3 to 4 minutes, stopping to scrape sides of bowl. Add eggs, one at a time, beating well after each addition. Beat in extracts. (Mixture may look slightly broken at this point, but batter will come together).

5. In a medium bowl, whisk together flour, baking powder, and remaining 1¼ teaspoons (3.75 grams) salt. In a small bowl, whisk together mascarpone and 1 tablespoon (15 grams) water. With mixer on low speed, gradually add flour mixture to butter mixture alternately with mascarpone mixture, beginning and ending with flour mixture, beating just until combined after each addition and stopping to scrape sides of bowl.
6. Using a fine-mesh sieve, strain chopped strawberries to get rid of any excess moisture. Fold strawberries into batter until combined.
7. Spray a 10-cup Bundt pan with baking spray with flour; using a pastry brush, spread any excess spray evenly in pan, blotting brush with a paper towel as needed. Spoon batter into prepared pan. Forcefully tap pan on a kitchen towel-lined counter several times to settle batter and release as many air bubbles as possible.
8. Bake until a wooden pick inserted near center comes out clean and an instant-read thermometer inserted near center registers 205°F (96°C), 50 minutes to 1 hour, rotating pan after 40 minutes of baking and loosely covering with foil to prevent excess browning, if necessary. Let cool in pan for 15 minutes. Invert cake onto a wire rack placed over a rimmed baking sheet.
9. Meanwhile, in a small saucepan, combine remaining ¼ cup (60 grams) water and remaining 2 tablespoons (24 grams) sugar. Bring to a boil over medium-high heat; cook, stirring frequently, until sugar dissolves. Remove from heat; stir in ¼ cup (65 grams) reserved roasted strawberry juice. (Reserve remaining juice for Strawberry Glaze.) Let cool for 5 minutes; generously brush all over warm cake until all of strawberry mixture is used up. Let cake cool completely.
10. Spoon Roasted Strawberry Glaze into a pastry bag; cut a ¼-inch opening in tip. Working quickly, drizzle glaze into and on ridges of cooled cake.

Note: *Roasting intensifies flavor and tenderizes fruit, even when it's not exactly in its prime. That said, you can also substitute 22 ounces (624 grams) frozen whole strawberries. Roast as directed, no thawing necessary. If your frozen berries don't yield enough strawberry juice for both the simple syrup and the glaze, substitute with water as needed.*

ROASTED STRAWBERRY GLAZE
Makes about ⅔ cup

1½   cups (180 grams) confectioners' sugar
3   tablespoons (48 grams) roasted strawberry juice (reserved from Roasted Strawberry-Mascarpone Bundt Cake)
1   tablespoon (14 grams) unsalted butter, melted
¼   teaspoon kosher salt

1. In a small bowl, whisk together all ingredients until smooth and well combined. Use immediately.

bake it a **BUNDT**LETTE

ROASTED STRAWBERRY-MASCARPONE BUNDTLETTES

Makes 6 Bundtlettes

1	pound (454 grams) fresh strawberries (see Notes) (halved or quartered if large)
¾	cup (150 grams) plus 3 tablespoons (36 grams) granulated sugar, divided
¾	teaspoon (2.25 grams) plus ⅛ teaspoon kosher salt, divided
6	tablespoons (84 grams) unsalted butter, softened
1	large egg (50 grams), room temperature
1	large egg yolk (19 grams), room temperature
½	teaspoon (2 grams) vanilla extract
¼	teaspoon (1 gram) almond extract
1¼	cups (156 grams) all-purpose flour
1½	teaspoons (7.5 grams) baking powder
⅓	cup (80 grams) mascarpone cheese, room temperature
2	tablespoons (30 grams) plus 1½ teaspoons (7.5 grams) water, room temperature and divided

Roasted Strawberry Glaze (recipe follows)

1. Preheat oven to 375°F (190°C). Line a rimmed baking sheet with parchment paper.

2. In an 8-inch square baking dish, stir together strawberries, 2 tablespoons (24 grams) sugar, and ⅛ teaspoon salt until well combined.

3. Bake until berries are very soft (they should provide no resistance when poked with a fork) and fragrant and have released ample juices, about 30 minutes, stirring every 10 minutes. Using a slotted spoon, transfer strawberries to prepared baking sheet. Reserve roasted strawberry juice in a 1-cup glass measuring cup or a small bowl. Let strawberries cool to room temperature; chop into ¼-inch pieces. Reduce oven temperature to 350°F (180°C).

4. In the bowl of a stand mixer fitted with the paddle attachment, beat butter and ¾ cup (150 grams) sugar at medium-low speed until fluffy, 3 to 4 minutes, stopping to scrape sides of bowl. Add egg and egg yolk, one at a time, beating well after each addition. Beat in extracts. (Mixture may look slightly broken at this point, but batter will come together.)

5. In a medium bowl, whisk together flour, baking powder, and remaining ¾ teaspoon (2.25 grams) salt. In a small bowl, whisk together mascarpone and 1½ teaspoons (7.5 grams) water. With mixer on low speed, gradually add flour mixture to butter mixture alternately with mascarpone mixture, beginning and ending with flour mixture, beating just until combined after each addition and stopping to scrape sides of bowl.

6. Using a fine-mesh sieve, strain chopped strawberries to get rid of any excess moisture. Fold strawberries into batter until combined.

7. Spray a 5-cup Bundtlette Pan (see Notes) with baking spray with flour; using a pastry brush, spread any excess spray evenly in wells of pan, blotting brush with a paper towel as needed. Spoon batter evenly into prepared wells. Forcefully tap pan on a kitchen towel-lined counter several times to settle batter and release as many air bubbles as possible.

8. Bake until a wooden pick inserted near center comes out clean and an instant-read thermometer inserted near center registers at least 205°F (96°C), 12 to 15 minutes. Let cool in pan for 15 minutes. Invert cakes onto a wire rack placed over a rimmed baking sheet.

9. Meanwhile, in a small microwave-safe bowl, stir together remaining 2 tablespoons (30 grams) water and remaining 1 tablespoon (12 grams) sugar. Heat on high in 10- to 20-second intervals, stirring between each, until sugar dissolves. Stir in 2 tablespoons (32 grams) reserved roasted strawberry juice. (Reserve remaining juice for Strawberry Glaze.) Let cool for 5 minutes; generously brush all over warm cakes until all of strawberry mixture is used up. Let cakes cool completely.

10. Spoon Roasted Strawberry Glaze into a pastry bag; cut a ¼-inch opening in tip. Working quickly, drizzle glaze into and on ridges of cooled cake.

Notes: *Roasting intensifies flavor and tenderizes fruit, even when it's not exactly in its prime. That said, you can also substitute 11 ounces (312 grams) frozen whole strawberries. Roast as directed, no thawing necessary. If your frozen berries don't yield enough strawberry juice for both the simple syrup and the glaze, substitute with water as needed.*

This recipe fits 5-cup-capacity Bundtlette Pans. For Bundtlette Pans with smaller capacities, fill wells only two-thirds to three-fourths full.

ROASTED STRAWBERRY GLAZE

Makes about ⅔ cup

1½	cups (180 grams) confectioners' sugar
3	tablespoons (48 grams) roasted strawberry juice (reserved from Roasted Strawberry-Mascarpone Bundtlettes)
1	tablespoon (14 grams) unsalted butter, melted
¼	teaspoon kosher salt

1. In a small bowl, whisk together all ingredients until smooth and well combined. Use immediately.

bake FROM SCRATCH
BUNDTOLOGY

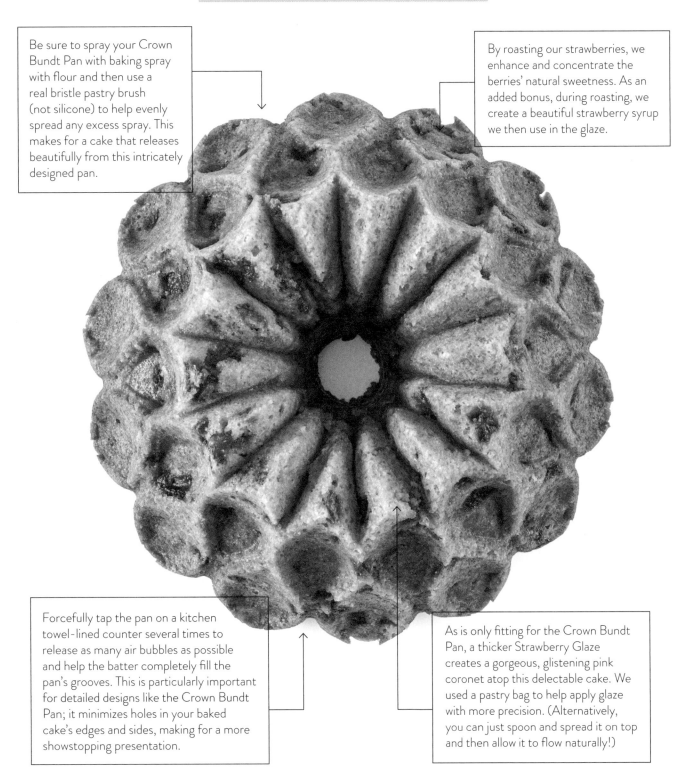

Be sure to spray your Crown Bundt Pan with baking spray with flour and then use a real bristle pastry brush (not silicone) to help evenly spread any excess spray. This makes for a cake that releases beautifully from this intricately designed pan.

By roasting our strawberries, we enhance and concentrate the berries' natural sweetness. As an added bonus, during roasting, we create a beautiful strawberry syrup we then use in the glaze.

Forcefully tap the pan on a kitchen towel-lined counter several times to release as many air bubbles as possible and help the batter completely fill the pan's grooves. This is particularly important for detailed designs like the Crown Bundt Pan; it minimizes holes in your baked cake's edges and sides, making for a more showstopping presentation.

As is only fitting for the Crown Bundt Pan, a thicker Strawberry Glaze creates a gorgeous, glistening pink coronet atop this delectable cake. We used a pastry bag to help apply glaze with more precision. (Alternatively, you can just spoon and spread it on top and then allow it to flow naturally!)

BLUEBERRY SWIRL POUND CAKE

Makes 1 (12-cup) Bundt cake

Lemon and blueberries are a match made in heaven, complementing each other in this simple, fresh cake beautifully. We love adding sour cream to the batter, which adds moisture and a wonderful rich flavor, leading to the most tender crumb.

1½ cups (340 grams) unsalted butter, softened
3 cups (600 grams) granulated sugar
6 large eggs (300 grams), room temperature
2 teaspoons (10 grams) lemon zest
1 teaspoon (4 grams) vanilla extract
3 cups (375 grams) all-purpose flour
1 teaspoon (3 grams) kosher salt
½ teaspoon (2.5 grams) baking soda
½ cup (120 grams) sour cream, room temperature
½ cup (140 grams) blueberry fruit spread*
Simple Glaze (recipe follows)

1. Preheat oven to 325°F (170°C).
2. In the bowl of a stand mixer fitted with the paddle attachment, beat butter and sugar at medium speed until light and fluffy, about 5 minutes, stopping to scrape sides of bowl. Add eggs, one at a time, beating well after each addition. Beat in lemon zest and vanilla.
3. In a medium bowl, whisk together flour, salt, and baking soda. With mixer on low speed, gradually add flour mixture to butter mixture alternately with sour cream, beginning and ending with flour mixture, beating until just combined after each addition.
4. Spray a 12-cup Bundt pan with baking spray with flour. Spoon half of batter (3½ cups or 847 grams) into prepared pan. Gently tap pan on kitchen towel-lined counter several times to release any air bubbles. Using the back of a spoon, make a ½-inch-deep, 1-inch-wide trench in center of batter in pan, leaving a ½-inch border around edges.
5. In a small bowl, stir together fruit spread and 3 tablespoons (45 grams) remaining batter. Spoon fruit spread mixture into trench. Using a knife, gently swirl fruit spread mixture into batter. Spoon remaining batter on top.
6. Bake until a wooden pick inserted near center comes out clean, 1 hour to 1 hour and 5 minutes. Let cool in pan for 15 minutes. Invert cake onto wire rack, and let cool completely. Drizzle Simple Glaze onto cake; let stand until set, 15 to 20 minutes. Cover and refrigerate for up to 3 days.

We used Bonne Maman Blueberry Fruit Spread.

SIMPLE GLAZE
Makes ⅓ cup

1 cup (120 grams) confectioners' sugar
1 tablespoon (15 grams) whole milk
1½ teaspoons (7.5 grams) fresh lemon juice
½ teaspoon (2 grams) vanilla extract

1. In a small bowl, whisk together all ingredients until combined.

JAM DOUGHNUT BUNDT

Makes 1 (10-cup) Bundt cake

Now you don't have to decide between a doughnut or cake! With its delicate, moist crumb, fruity raspberry jam filling, and sweet pink glaze speckled with sprinkles, this festive cake combines all the qualities of doughnuts in one crowd-pleasing Bundt!

1¼ cups (284 grams) unsalted butter, softened
¾   cup (150 grams) granulated sugar
⅔   cup (147 grams) firmly packed light brown sugar
5   large eggs (250 grams), room temperature
2   teaspoons (12 grams) vanilla bean paste
2½ cups (313 grams) all-purpose flour
2   teaspoons (10 grams) baking powder
1½ teaspoons (3 grams) ground nutmeg
1   teaspoon (3 grams) kosher salt
¼   cup (60 grams) sour cream, room temperature
3   tablespoons (45 grams) whole milk, room temperature
⅓   cup (108 grams) seedless raspberry jam
6   drops red liquid food coloring* (optional)
Pink Doughnut Glaze (recipe follows)
Garnish: rainbow sprinkles

1. Preheat oven to 350°F (180°C).
2. In the bowl of a stand mixer fitted with the paddle attachment, beat butter and sugars at medium speed until light and fluffy, 5 to 7 minutes, stopping to scrape sides of bowl. Add eggs, one at a time, beating well after each addition. Beat in vanilla bean paste.
3. In a medium bowl, whisk together flour, baking powder, nutmeg, and salt. In a small bowl, stir together sour cream and milk. With mixer on low speed, gradually add flour mixture to butter mixture alternately with sour cream mixture, beginning and ending with flour mixture, beating just until combined after each addition and stopping to scrape sides of bowl.

4. Spray a 10-cup Nordic Ware Swirl Bundt Pan with baking spray with flour. Spoon 3 cups (684 grams) batter into prepared pan. Tap pan on a kitchen towel-lined counter several times to settle batter and release any air bubbles.
5. In a small bowl, whisk together jam, food coloring (if using), and 3 tablespoons (42 grams) remaining batter.
6. Using the back of a spoon, make a 1¼- to 1½-inch-wide, ½-inch-deep trench in center of batter in pan. Spoon ¾ cup (170 grams) batter into a pastry bag; cut a ½-inch opening in tip. Pipe a border of batter, tracing outer and inner edges of pan. Spoon and pipe alternating small dollops of batter and large dollops of jam mixture into trench in pan. After completing 1 ring in pan, pipe batter on top of jam dollops and vice versa until both are used up. Drag a wooden pick through centers of dollops a few times to swirl together, being careful to stay within piped border. Pipe and gently spread remaining batter on top, covering jam mixture. Do not tap pan.
7. Bake until a wooden pick inserted near center comes out clean and an instant-read thermometer inserted near center registers 200°F (93°C), 50 to 56 minutes, rotating pan and loosely covering with foil after 25 to 30 minutes of baking to prevent excess browning. Let cool in pan for 15 minutes. Invert cake onto a wire rack, and let cool completely.
8. Spoon Pink Doughnut Glaze into a pastry bag; cut a ½-inch opening in tip. Pipe glaze onto cooled cake. Garnish with sprinkles, if desired. Any leftovers can be stored in an airtight container for 2 days at room temperature or 3 to 5 days in the refrigerator. Let refrigerated cake come back to room temperature before serving.

*We used McCormick Red Food Color.

PINK DOUGHNUT GLAZE

Makes about ¾ cup

2   cups (240 grams) confectioners' sugar
3   tablespoons (42 grams) unsalted butter, melted
3   drops red liquid food coloring
½   teaspoon (2 grams) vanilla extract
¼   teaspoon kosher salt
2 to 3 tablespoons (30 to 45 grams) whole milk, room temperature

1. In a medium bowl, stir together confectioners' sugar, melted butter, food coloring, vanilla, and salt. Add enough milk to make a thick icing that falls off spatula in ribbons. Use immediately.

CHOCOLATE-GLAZED PEANUT BUTTER-BANANA CAKE

Makes 1 (10-cup) Bundt cake

Creamy peanut butter and ripe bananas pair perfectly with a crowning glory of chocolaty glaze, creating an irresistible treat that will have you coming back for more!

1   cup (200 grams) granulated sugar
¾   cup (168 grams) neutral oil
⅔   cup (185 grams) mashed very ripe banana (about 2 medium bananas)
½   cup (110 grams) firmly packed light brown sugar
½   cup (128 grams) creamy peanut butter
2   large eggs (100 grams), room temperature
2   teaspoons (8 grams) vanilla extract
1   cup (240 grams) whole buttermilk, room temperature
2½   cups (313 grams) all-purpose flour
1   teaspoon (5 grams) baking powder
1   teaspoon (3 grams) kosher salt
¼   teaspoon (1.25 grams) baking soda
Shiny Chocolate Glaze (recipe follows)

1. Preheat oven to 325°F (170°C).
2. In a large bowl, whisk together granulated sugar, oil, banana, brown sugar, and peanut butter until well combined, about 1 minute. Add eggs and vanilla, and whisk until well combined. Whisk in buttermilk.
3. In a medium bowl, whisk together flour, baking powder, salt, and baking soda. Gradually whisk flour mixture into sugar mixture until just combined, stopping to scrape sides of bowl. (Do not overmix.)
4. Spray a 10-cup Bundt pan with baking spray with flour. Pour batter into prepared pan. Tap pan on a kitchen towel-lined counter 4 to 5 times to settle batter and release any air bubbles.
5. Bake until golden brown, a wooden pick inserted near center comes out clean, and an instant-read thermometer inserted near center registers 205°F (96°C), 50 to 55 minutes, covering with foil after 40 minutes of baking to prevent excess browning. Let cool in pan for 15 minutes. Invert cake onto a wire rack, and let cool completely.
6. Spoon Shiny Chocolate Glaze onto cooled cake.

SHINY CHOCOLATE GLAZE
Makes about ¾ cup

4   ounces (113 grams) 60% to 70% cacao bittersweet chocolate, finely chopped
½   cup (120 grams) heavy whipping cream
1   tablespoon (21 grams) light corn syrup

1. In a small bowl, place chocolate.
2. In a small saucepan, heat cream and corn syrup over medium heat, stirring occasionally, until steaming. (Do not boil.) Immediately pour over chocolate. Let stand for 5 minutes. Starting in center of bowl, slowly stir with a rubber spatula until well combined. Use immediately. (The glaze thickens as it cools. If you need to soften the glaze again, microwave on high in 10-second intervals, stirring between each, until fluid and smooth. Or place the bowl in warm water, and let stand, stirring occasionally, until fluid and smooth).

BANANAS FOSTER BUNDT CAKE

Makes 1 (10-cup) Bundt cake

Ripe bananas give the cake its signature fruity flavor, and toasted pecans provide the perfect nutty note to balance out the sweetness of the cake. And as if this dessert couldn't get any more decadent, we topped it with an extra helping of ice cream, a sprinkle of toasted pecans, and brûléed bananas.

1¼	cups (300 grams) finely mashed ripe banana (3 to 4 large bananas)
1	cup (210 grams) melted vanilla ice cream*, room temperature
⅔	cup (147 grams) firmly packed dark brown sugar
⅔	cup (149 grams) vegetable oil
½	cup (120 grams) sour cream, room temperature
¼	cup (50 grams) granulated sugar
3	large eggs (150 grams), room temperature
1	tablespoon (15 grams) dark rum (see Notes)
1	teaspoon (6 grams) vanilla bean paste
3	cups (375 grams) plus 1 teaspoon (3 grams) all-purpose flour, divided
2	teaspoons (10 grams) baking powder
1¼	teaspoons (3.75 grams) kosher salt
1	teaspoon (5 grams) baking soda
1	teaspoon (2 grams) ground cinnamon
½	cup (57 grams) finely chopped toasted pecans

Brown Sugar Rum Sauce (recipe follows)
Garnish: vanilla ice cream, chopped toasted pecans, brûléed bananas (see Notes)

1. Preheat oven to 350°F (180°C).
2. In a large bowl, whisk together mashed banana, melted ice cream, brown sugar, oil, sour cream, granulated sugar, eggs, rum, and vanilla bean paste until well combined, stopping to scrape sides of bowl.
3. In a large bowl, whisk together 3 cups (375 grams) flour, baking powder, salt, baking soda, and cinnamon. Gradually stir flour mixture into banana mixture just until some flour streaks remain.
4. In a small bowl, stir together finely chopped pecans and remaining 1 teaspoon (3 grams) flour. Fold pecan mixture into batter just until combined.

5. Spray a 10-cup Bundt pan with baking spray with flour. Pour batter into prepared pan. Forcefully tap pan on a kitchen towel-lined counter several times to settle batter and release as many air bubbles as possible.
6. Bake for 35 minutes. Rotate pan, and loosely cover with foil; bake until a wooden pick inserted near center comes out clean and an instant-read thermometer registers at least 200°F (93°C), 25 to 30 minutes more. (Cake will bake with a slightly rounded top.) Let cool in pan for 20 minutes. Invert cake onto a wire rack, and let cool completely.
7. Using a serrated knife, level bottom of cooled cake. Place cake, cut side down, on a 12-inch rimmed serving platter. Using a spoon, drizzle Brown Sugar Rum Sauce into and over grooves of cake as desired. Pour ½ cup (140 grams) Brown Sugar Rum Sauce into center of cake; garnish with ice cream, chopped pecans, and brûléed bananas, if desired. Drizzle with more Brown Sugar Rum Sauce; serve immediately with any extra sauce.

When selecting a brand of ice cream, we opted for a brand that does not include egg yolks in the ingredient list. Using an ice cream that is made with egg yolks can make a denser and less tender cake.

Notes: For an alcohol-free option, you can substitute the rum in the cake and the sauce with rum extract to taste or omit it all together.

To brûlée bananas, place ¼-inch-thick banana slices on a heatproof baking sheet. Sprinkle with 1 tablespoon (12 grams) granulated sugar. Using a handheld kitchen torch, carefully and lightly brown sugar.

BROWN SUGAR RUM SAUCE
Makes about 2⅓ cups

1	cup (200 grams) melted vanilla ice cream
⅔	cup (147 grams) firmly packed dark brown sugar
½	cup (113 grams) unsalted butter, cubed and softened
⅓	cup (113 grams) dark corn syrup
3	tablespoons (36 grams) granulated sugar
1	teaspoon (3 grams) kosher salt
¼	teaspoon ground cinnamon
3	tablespoons (45 grams) dark rum

1. In a medium saucepan, stir together ice cream, brown sugar, butter, corn syrup, granulated sugar, salt, and cinnamon. Bring to a boil over medium-high heat; reduce heat to medium-low, and simmer, stirring frequently, for 2 minutes. Remove from heat; stir in rum. Return to heat, and bring to a boil over medium-high heat; cook, stirring frequently, for 1 minute. Remove from heat, and pour into a small heatproof bowl. Let cool for 15 minutes before using, stirring occasionally.

BANANAS FOSTER BUNDTLETTES

Makes 6 Bundtlettes

⅔   cup (160 grams) finely mashed ripe banana (about 2 large bananas)
½   cup (100 grams) melted vanilla ice cream (see Notes), room temperature
⅓   cup (73 grams) firmly packed dark brown sugar
⅓   cup (75 grams) vegetable oil
¼   cup (60 grams) sour cream, room temperature
1   large egg (50 grams), room temperature
1   large egg yolk (19 grams), room temperature
2   tablespoons (24 grams) granulated sugar
1½ teaspoons (7.5 grams) dark rum (see Notes)
½   teaspoon (3 grams) vanilla bean paste
1½ cups (188 grams) plus ½ teaspoon (1.5 grams) all-purpose flour, divided
1   teaspoon (5 grams) baking powder
¾   teaspoon (2.25 grams) kosher salt
½   teaspoon (2.5 grams) baking soda
½   teaspoon (1 gram) ground cinnamon
¼   cup (28 grams) finely chopped toasted pecans
Brown Sugar Rum Sauce (recipe follows)
Garnish: vanilla ice cream, chopped toasted pecans, brûléed bananas (see Notes)

1. Preheat oven to 350°F (180°C).
2. In a large bowl, whisk together mashed banana, melted ice cream, brown sugar, oil, sour cream, egg, egg yolk, granulated sugar, rum, and vanilla bean paste until well combined, stopping to scrape sides of bowl.
3. In a large bowl, whisk together 1½ cups (188 grams) flour, baking powder, salt, baking soda, and cinnamon. Gradually stir flour mixture into banana mixture just until some flour streaks remain.
4. In a small bowl, stir together finely chopped pecans and remaining ½ teaspoon (1.5 grams) flour. Fold pecan mixture into batter just until combined.
5. Spray a 4- to 5-cup Bundtlette pan with baking spray with flour. Divide batter among prepared wells. Forcefully tap pan on a kitchen towel-lined counter several times to settle batter and release as many air bubbles as possible.

6. Bake until a wooden pick inserted near center comes out clean, 12 to 18 minutes. (Cakes will bake with a slightly rounded top.) Let cool in pan for 20 minutes. Invert cakes onto a wire rack, and let cool completely.
7. Using a serrated knife, level bottom of cooled Bundtlettes. Place, cut side down, on a large rimmed serving platter. Using a spoon, drizzle Brown Sugar Rum Sauce over and into center of cakes as desired; garnish with ice cream, chopped pecans, and brûléed bananas, if desired. Drizzle with more Brown Sugar Rum Sauce; serve immediately with any extra sauce.

Notes: *When selecting a brand of ice cream, we opt for a brand that does not include egg yolks in the ingredient list. Using an ice cream that is made with egg yolks can make a denser and less tender cake.*

For an alcohol-free option, you can substitute the rum in the cake and the sauce with rum extract to taste or omit it all together.

To brûlée bananas, place ¼-inch-thick banana slices on a heatproof baking sheet. Sprinkle with 1 tablespoon (12 grams) granulated sugar. Using a handheld kitchen torch, carefully and lightly brown sugar.

BROWN SUGAR RUM SAUCE
Makes about 1 cup

½   cup (100 grams) melted vanilla ice cream
⅓   cup (73 grams) firmly packed dark brown sugar
¼   cup (57 grams) unsalted butter, cubed and softened
2½ tablespoons (53 grams) dark corn syrup
1½ tablespoons (18 grams) granulated sugar
½   teaspoon (1.5 grams) kosher salt
⅛   teaspoon ground cinnamon
1½ tablespoons (22.5 grams) dark rum

1. In a small saucepan, stir together ice cream, brown sugar, butter, corn syrup, granulated sugar, salt, and cinnamon. Bring to a boil over medium-high heat; reduce heat to medium-low, and simmer, stirring frequently, for 2 minutes. Remove from heat; stir in rum. Return to heat, and bring to a boil over medium-high heat; cook, stirring frequently, for 1 minute. Remove from heat, and pour into a small heatproof bowl. Let cool for 15 minutes before using, stirring occasionally.

Inspired by a classic bananas Foster pairing, we mixed vanilla ice cream into our batter and brown sugar sauce for added sweetness, richness, and flavor. Additional scoops in the center make for a fun, decadent presentation.

Beyond the Jubilee Bundt Pan's geometric grooves, we poured more sauce in this Bundt's center for a luscious surprise once sliced.

This cake bakes slightly rounded like banana bread. To ensure our sauce stays in the center, we used a serrated knife to shave off this rounded bottom and allow the cake to sit flat. Any scraps can be saved for snacks or garnish.

Dark rum infuses this Bundt with iconic bananas Foster flavor, but for an alcohol-free option, swap in rum extract to taste or omit it all together. Since extract is more potent, start with ½ to 1 teaspoon (2 to 4 grams), taste, and add more as needed.

MARBLED STRAWBERRY BUNDT CAKE

Makes 1 (10-cup) Bundt cake

Topped with a Buttermilk Glaze that balances between tart and sweet and sliced fresh strawberries, this cake is sure to be a summertime sensation.

1	cup plus 2 tablespoons (255 grams) unsalted butter, softened
1⅔	cups (333 grams) granulated sugar
4	large eggs (200 grams), room temperature
2	teaspoons (8 grams) vanilla extract
2¼	cups (281 grams) unbleached cake flour*, divided
½	teaspoon (2.5 grams) baking powder, divided
½	teaspoon kosher salt, divided
6	tablespoons (90 grams) whole buttermilk, room temperature
⅔	cup (160 grams) Roasted Strawberry Purée (recipe follows)

6 to 7 drops red liquid food coloring*
Buttermilk Glaze (recipe follows)
Garnish: fresh strawberries

1. Preheat oven to 325°F (170°C).
2. In the bowl of a stand mixer fitted with the paddle attachment, beat butter and sugar at medium speed until light and fluffy, about 5 minutes, stopping to scrape sides of bowl. Add eggs, one at a time, beating well after each addition. Beat in vanilla. (Mixture may look slightly broken, but batter will come together.) Transfer half of butter mixture (about 402 grams) to a medium bowl.
3. In a small bowl, whisk together 1¼ cups (156 grams) flour, ¼ teaspoon (1.25 grams) baking powder, and ¼ teaspoon salt. Fold flour mixture into half of butter mixture alternately with buttermilk, beginning and ending with flour mixture, folding just until combined. Set aside.
4. In another small bowl, whisk together remaining 1 cup (125 grams) flour, remaining ¼ teaspoon (1.25 grams) baking powder, and remaining ¼ teaspoon salt. In another small bowl, stir together Roasted Strawberry Purée and food coloring. Fold flour mixture into remaining butter mixture alternately with strawberry mixture, beginning and ending with flour mixture, folding just until combined.
5. Spray a 10-cup Bundt pan with cooking spray. Using a pastry brush, spread any excess spray evenly in pan, blotting brush with a paper towel as needed, and lightly flour pan, tapping out any excess to make a very thin layer.

6. Spoon plain and strawberry batters into separate large pastry bags; cut a ½-inch opening in each tip. Pipe random small and medium dollops of batter in a ring in bottom of prepared pan. Repeat procedure, piping strawberry batter on top of vanilla batter and vanilla batter on top of strawberry batter to create a checkerboard-like pattern until all of batter is used up. Using a butter knife, swirl batters using a figure eight motion, being careful not to touch bottom and sides of pan. Firmly tap pan on a kitchen towel-lined counter several times to settle batters and release any air bubbles.
7. Bake until a wooden pick inserted near center comes out clean, 52 to 58 minutes, rotating pan halfway through baking and loosely covering with foil during final 5 to 6 minutes of baking to prevent excess browning. Let cool in pan for 10 minutes. Invert cake onto a wire rack, and let cool completely.
8. Transfer cooled cake to a serving plate, and spoon Buttermilk Glaze on top. Garnish with strawberries, if desired. Refrigerate in an airtight container for up to 5 days; let come to room temperature before serving.

We used King Arthur Unbleached Cake Flour and McCormick Red Food Color.

PRO TIP
Place an oven-safe wire rack directly on your oven rack to create a sturdy, crosshatched surface to help keep the Bundt pan level and stable while baking.

ROASTED STRAWBERRY PURÉE
Makes about ¾ cup

15	ounces (425 grams) ½- to ¾-inch-thick chopped fresh strawberries
2	tablespoons (24 grams) granulated sugar

1. Preheat oven to 350°F (180°C). Line a rimmed baking sheet with parchment paper.
2. On prepared pan, toss together strawberries and sugar until combined; spread in a single layer.
3. Bake until berries are very soft and fragrant and juices are deep red and starting to thicken at edges of pan, 20 to 25 minutes, stirring every 5 to 10 minutes. Let cool completely on pan.
4. Using a fine-mesh sieve, thoroughly strain strawberries. Reserve any juice for another use. (See Note.)
5. Place strained strawberries in the work bowl of a food processor; process until puréed, stopping to scrape sides of bowl.

Note: *Any extra strawberry purée or juice makes a great addition to smoothies, cocktails, yogurt, and more.*

Buttermilk Glaze
Makes about ⅔ cup

1¼ cups (150 grams) confectioners' sugar
2   tablespoons (30 grams) whole buttermilk
¼   teaspoon (1 gram) vanilla extract

1. In a small bowl, stir together all ingredients until smooth and well combined. Use immediately.

A MARBLING MODEL
How to create the signature swirl of this marbled beauty

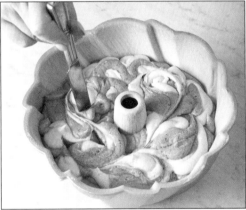

1. Spoon plain and strawberry batters into separate large pastry bags; cut a ½-inch opening in each tip. Pipe random small and medium dollops of batter in a ring in bottom of prepared pan. Repeat procedure, piping strawberry batter on top of vanilla batter and vanilla batter on top of strawberry batter to create a checkerboard-like pattern until all of batter is used up. Using a butter knife, swirl batters using a figure-8 motion, being careful not to touch bottom and sides of pan. Firmly tap pan on a kitchen towel-lined counter several times to settle batters and release any air bubbles.

KEY LIME CAKE

Makes 1 (6-cup) cake

This cake starts with a graham cracker-laced batter that's buttery and rich like your favorite Key lime pie crust but bakes into a gorgeously fluffy, tender crumb. A quick pass of a kitchen torch over the meringue creates a slight toasted marshmallow flavor. Though these flavors may be familiar, this cake is sure to wow.

½ cup (113 grams) unsalted butter, softened
1 cup (200 grams) granulated sugar
2 large eggs (100 grams), room temperature
1⅔ cups (125 grams) all-purpose flour
2 tablespoons (16 grams) finely ground graham cracker crumbs, sifted
1 teaspoon (5 grams) baking powder
¾ teaspoon (2.25 grams) kosher salt
⅔ cup (160 grams) whole milk, room temperature
1 teaspoon (4 grams) vanilla extract
Key Lime Custard (recipe follows)
Swiss Meringue (recipe follows)

1. Preheat oven to 325°F (170°C).
2. In the bowl of a stand mixer fitted with the paddle attachment, beat butter and sugar at medium speed until fluffy, 3 to 4 minutes, stopping to scrape sides of bowl. Add eggs, one at a time, beating well after each addition.
3. In a medium bowl, whisk together flour, graham cracker crumbs, baking powder, and salt. In a small bowl, whisk together milk and vanilla. With mixer on low speed, gradually add flour mixture to butter mixture alternately with milk mixture, beginning and ending with flour mixture, beating just until combined after each addition.
4. Spray a Nordic Ware 6-Cup Charlotte Cake Pan with baking spray with flour. Using a pastry brush, spread any excess spray in pan, blotting brush with a paper towel as needed. Spread batter into prepared pan. Tap pan on a kitchen towel-lined counter several times to settle batter and release any air bubbles.
5. Bake until golden and a wooden pick inserted in center comes out clean, 35 to 40 minutes. Let cool in pan for 10 minutes. Invert cake onto a wire rack, and let cool completely.
6. Transfer cake to a serving plate. Fill with Key Lime Custard, spreading with an offset spatula.
7. Place Swiss Meringue in a large pastry bag fitted with a ½-inch open star piping tip (Ateco #825). Pipe meringue as desired. Using a handheld kitchen torch, carefully brown meringue as desired. Serve immediately.

KEY LIME CUSTARD
Makes about 1½ cups

4 large egg yolks (74 grams)
1½ teaspoons (4.5 grams) cornstarch
1 cup (306 grams) sweetened condensed milk
1 teaspoon (2 grams) packed lime zest
6 tablespoons (90 grams) Key lime juice (from bottle)

1. In a medium saucepan, whisk together egg yolks and cornstarch. Whisk in condensed milk and lime zest and juice until smooth. Bring to a boil over medium heat, whisking constantly. Cook, whisking constantly, until thickened and smooth, 1 to 2 minutes. Pour into a heatproof bowl, and cover with plastic wrap, pressing wrap directly onto surface of custard to prevent a skin from forming. Refrigerate until completely cooled.

SWISS MERINGUE
Makes about 1 cup

½ cup (100 grams) granulated sugar
2 large egg whites (60 grams)

1. In the heatproof bowl of a stand mixer, whisk together sugar and egg whites by hand. Place bowl over a saucepan of simmering water. Cook, whisking frequently, until sugar completely dissolves and an instant-read thermometer registers 120°F (49°C) to 130°F (54°C).
2. Carefully return bowl to stand mixer. Using the whisk attachment, beat at high speed until stiff peaks form and bowl is cool to the touch, 2 to 3 minutes. Use immediately.

HONEY-BLACKBERRY CORNMEAL BUNDT

Makes 1 (10-cup) Bundt cake

This Bundt unleashes the power of goat milk with its naturally creamy texture and mildly sweet flavor. No access to goat milk? Whole buttermilk can be used in its place, adding tenderness and a hint of acidity to the sweet crumb. Whether it's the crave-worthy flavor of cornmeal or delightful bites of blackberry, this Bundt will have you coming back for more.

1⅓   cups (303 grams) unsalted butter, melted
¾   cup (150 grams) granulated sugar
½   cup (170 grams) plus 2 tablespoons (42 grams) clover honey, divided
⅓   cup (80 grams) whole goat milk or whole buttermilk, room temperature
4   large eggs (200 grams), room temperature
1   large egg yolk (19 grams), room temperature
4   teaspoons (8 grams) packed lemon zest
2   tablespoons (30 grams) fresh lemon juice
1⅔   cups (225 grams) plain yellow cornmeal
1½   cups (188 grams) plus 1 tablespoon (8 grams) all-purpose flour, divided
1   teaspoon (3 grams) kosher salt
½   teaspoon (2.5 grams) baking powder
¼   teaspoon (1.25 grams) baking soda
8   ounces (226 grams) fresh blackberries, halved (about 1⅔ cups)
Garnish: clover honey

1. Preheat oven to 300°F (150°C). Place a heatproof wire rack directly on oven rack, creating a sturdy, metal, crosshatched surface to help keep pan level.
2. In a large bowl, whisk together melted butter, sugar, ½ cup (170 grams) honey, goat's milk or buttermilk, eggs, egg yolk, and lemon zest and juice.
3. In a medium bowl, whisk together cornmeal, 1½ cups (188 grams) flour, salt, baking powder, and baking soda. Gradually whisk flour mixture into butter mixture just until some bits of flour remain.
4. In a small bowl, toss together blackberries and remaining 1 tablespoon (8 grams) flour. Fold blackberry mixture into batter just until combined.
5. Spray a 10-cup Bundt pan with baking spray with flour. Using a ¼-cup spring-loaded scoop, scoop batter into prepared pan. Forcefully tap pan on a kitchen towel-lined counter several times to settle batter and release any air bubbles.
6. Bake for 40 minutes. Rotate pan, and loosely cover with foil to prevent excess browning, if necessary. Bake until a wooden pick inserted near center comes out clean and an instant-read thermometer inserted near center registers 200°F (93°C), 30 to 40 minutes more. Let cool in pan for 10 minutes. Invert cake onto a wire rack placed over a rimmed baking sheet.
7. In a small microwave-safe bowl, heat remaining 2 tablespoons (42 grams) honey on high in 10-second intervals, stirring between each, until loose and fluid. Quickly and carefully brush onto warm cake. Let cool completely.
8. Transfer cooled cake to a serving plate. Garnish with honey, if desired.

bake it a BUNDTLETTE

HONEY-BLACKBERRY CORNMEAL BUNDTLETTES

Makes 6 Bundtlettes

⅔ cup (150 grams) unsalted butter, melted
⅓ cup (67 grams) granulated sugar
¼ cup (85 grams) plus 2 tablespoons (42 grams) clover honey, divided
2 large eggs (100 grams), room temperature
3 tablespoons (45 grams) whole goat milk or whole buttermilk, room temperature
2 teaspoons (3 grams) lemon zest
1 tablespoon (15 grams) fresh lemon juice
¾ cup plus 1 tablespoon (113 grams) plain yellow cornmeal
¾ cup (94 grams) plus 1½ teaspoons (4.5 grams) all-purpose flour, divided
½ teaspoon (1.5 grams) kosher salt
¼ teaspoon (1.25 grams) baking powder
⅛ teaspoon baking soda
4 ounces (113 grams) fresh blackberries, quartered (about a heaping ¾ cup)
Garnish: clover honey

1. Preheat oven to 300°F (150°C).
2. In a large bowl, whisk together melted butter, sugar, ¼ cup (85 grams) honey, eggs, goat's milk or buttermilk, and lemon zest and juice.
3. In a medium bowl, whisk together cornmeal, ¾ cup (94 grams) flour, salt, baking powder, and baking soda. Gradually whisk flour mixture into butter mixture just until some bits of flour remain.
4. In a small bowl, toss together blackberries and remaining 1½ teaspoons (4.5 grams) flour. Fold blackberry mixture into batter just until combined.
5. Spray a 4- or 5-cup Bundtlette pan with baking spray with flour. Using a 1½-teaspoon spring-loaded scoop, divide batter among prepared wells. Forcefully tap pan on a kitchen towel-lined counter several times to settle batter and release any air bubbles.
6. Bake until a wooden pick inserted near center comes out clean, 20 to 25 minutes. Let cool in pan for 10 minutes. Invert cakes onto a wire rack placed over a rimmed baking sheet.
7. In a small microwave-safe bowl, heat remaining 2 tablespoons (42 grams) honey on high in 10-second intervals, stirring between each, until loose and fluid. Quickly and carefully brush over warm cakes. Let cakes cool completely. Garnish with honey, if desired.

This fluid, cornmeal-flecked batter easily fills the Bundt pan's intricate design and bakes into a gorgeous golden coronet.

A simple honey drizzle makes for a showstopping finish that also allows the pan's design to shine.

This summery Bundt is beautifully easy and super customizable. Swap buttermilk for goat milk or substitute the same weight of fresh raspberries or blueberries for blackberries for a different, yet still delicious, twist.

Tossing the blackberries in flour before folding them into the batter helps them stay suspended in every lovely slice.

A ¼-cup spring-loaded scoop makes transferring the batter into the pan an absolute breeze.

FIG AND APPLE DAPPLE BUNDT CAKE

Makes 1 (15-cup) Bundt cake

Complete with notes of caramel, spice, sweet fall fruits, and nutty pecans, this harvest-fresh bake promises a sweet taste of fall in every bite. Reminiscent of caramel apples and crisp autumn days spent at the apple orchard, it's the perfect cake to kick off the fall baking season.

1⅓ cups (267 grams) granulated sugar
¾ cup (160 grams) vegetable oil
⅔ cup (150 grams) unsalted butter, melted
⅓ cup (73 grams) firmly packed dark brown sugar
3 large eggs (150 grams), room temperature
1 tablespoon (13 grams) vanilla extract
3 cups (375 grams) plus 2 tablespoons (16 grams) all-purpose flour, divided
2 teaspoons (4 grams) ground cinnamon
1 teaspoon (5 grams) baking soda
1 teaspoon (3 grams) kosher salt
½ teaspoon (1 gram) ground nutmeg
¼ teaspoon ground allspice
3 cups (375 grams) ⅓- to ½-inch-chopped peeled Golden Delicious apples
1 cup (113 grams) chopped toasted pecans
1 cup (165 grams) chopped dried Mission figs*
Quick Caramel Sauce (recipe follows)
Garnish: chopped toasted pecans

1. Preheat oven to 350°F (180°C).
2. In the bowl of a stand mixer fitted with the paddle attachment, beat granulated sugar, oil, melted butter, brown sugar, eggs, and vanilla at medium-low speed until well combined, about 2 minutes, stopping to scrape sides of bowl.
3. In a medium bowl, whisk together 3 cups (375 grams) flour, cinnamon, baking soda, salt, nutmeg, and allspice. With mixer on low speed, gradually add flour mixture to sugar mixture, beating until combined and stopping to scrape sides of bowl. (Batter will be quite thick.)
4. In another medium bowl, stir together apples, pecans, figs, and remaining 2 tablespoons (16 grams) flour. Fold apple mixture into batter.
5. Spray a 15-cup Bundt pan with baking spray with flour. Spoon batter into prepared pan. Tap pan on a kitchen towel-lined counter several times to settle batter and release any air bubbles.

6. Bake until a wooden pick inserted near center comes out clean, 1 hour to 1 hour and 10 minutes, rotating pan halfway through baking and loosely covering with foil to prevent excess browning, if necessary.
7. Poke hot cake all over with a wooden skewer; pour ¾ cup (about 200 grams) Quick Caramel Sauce onto cake in pan, spreading evenly with a small offset spatula. Let cake cool completely in pan on a wire rack. (See Note.) Transfer remaining Quick Caramel Sauce to a small microwave-safe bowl; cover and refrigerate.
8. When ready to serve, using a small offset spatula, gently loosen cooled cake from center and edges of pan. Invert cake onto a cake plate.
9. Heat remaining Quick Caramel Sauce on high in 10-second intervals, stirring between each, until melted and smooth. Drizzle sauce onto cooled cake. Garnish with pecans, if desired.

*We used Orchard Choice California Dried Mission Figs from Valley Fig Growers.

Note: *This cake will take several hours to cool completely and only gets better with age. If you make it in the morning, it will be fully cooled by the end of the day. If you make it in the evening, be prepared to let it cool overnight.*

QUICK CARAMEL SAUCE
Makes about 1½ cups

1 cup (220 grams) firmly packed dark brown sugar
¾ cup (170 grams) unsalted butter, softened
¼ cup (60 grams) heavy whipping cream
½ teaspoon (1.5 grams) kosher salt
2 tablespoons (30 grams) dark spiced rum
1 teaspoon (4 grams) vanilla extract

1. In a medium saucepan, combine brown sugar, butter, cream, and salt. Bring to a boil over medium-high heat, stirring frequently; cook, stirring constantly, for 2 minutes. Remove from heat; stir in rum and vanilla.

CINNAMON BLUEBERRY BUNDT CAKE

Makes 1 (10-cup) Bundt cake

Blending warm cinnamon with bright blueberries, this simple cake is a Bundt-size take on a bakery-style blueberry muffin.

1   cup (125 grams) plus 1 tablespoon (8 grams) all-purpose flour, divided
1   cup (123 grams) cake flour
2   teaspoons (4 grams) ground cinnamon
1   teaspoon (5 grams) baking powder
1   teaspoon (3 grams) kosher salt
¼   teaspoon (1.25 grams) baking soda
½   cup (113 grams) unsalted butter, melted
⅓   cup (67 grams) granulated sugar
⅓   cup (73 grams) firmly packed light brown sugar
¼   cup (85 grams) maple syrup
2   large eggs (100 grams)
2   teaspoons (2 grams) lemon zest (about 1 small lemon)
1   teaspoon (4 grams) vanilla extract
⅓   cup (80 grams) plain Greek yogurt
1½   cups (210 grams) frozen blueberries
Vanilla Buttermilk Glaze (recipe follows)

1. Preheat oven to 350°F (180°C).
2. In a medium bowl, whisk together 1 cup (125 grams) all-purpose flour, cake flour, cinnamon, baking powder, salt, and baking soda.
3. In a large bowl, whisk together melted butter, sugars, maple syrup, eggs, lemon zest, and vanilla. Whisk in yogurt. Add flour mixture, and whisk just until dry ingredients are moistened.
4. In a small bowl, toss together blueberries and remaining 1 tablespoon (8 grams) all-purpose flour. Fold blueberry mixture into batter.
5. Generously spray a 10-cup Bundt pan with baking spray with flour. Spread batter into prepared pan, smoothing with an offset spatula. Firmly tap pan on a kitchen towel-lined counter several times to settle batter.
6. Bake until a wooden pick inserted near center comes out clean, about 50 minutes, covering with foil halfway through baking to prevent excess browning. Let cool in pan for 15 minutes. Using a small offset spatula, gently loosen cake from center and edges of pan. Invert cake onto a wire rack, and let cool completely. Spoon and spread Vanilla Buttermilk Glaze onto cooled cake as desired. Refrigerate in an airtight container for up to 3 days.

VANILLA BUTTERMILK GLAZE

Makes about ⅔ cup

1¾   cups (210 grams) confectioners' sugar
3   tablespoons (45 grams) whole buttermilk
1   tablespoon (14 grams) unsalted butter, melted
½   teaspoon (2 grams) vanilla extract
¼   teaspoon kosher salt

1. In a medium bowl, whisk together all ingredients until smooth. Use immediately.

JUST BECAUSE

YOU DON'T NEED A SPECIAL OCCASION TO
ENJOY THESE SLICES OF DELICIOUSNESS

CONFETTI BUNDT CAKE

Makes 1 (10-cup) Bundt cake

We took the vanilla Bundt cake to new heights with our confetti cake, covered with a rosy strawberry glaze and flecked with bright rainbow sprinkles. With a light, spongy crumb surrounded by a golden-brown exterior, this flirty cake is ready for all your summer celebrations!

1⅓   cups (266 grams) granulated sugar
2   large eggs (100 grams), room temperature
½   cup (112 grams) vegetable oil
½   cup (120 grams) whole milk, room temperature
2   tablespoons (30 grams) sour cream, room temperature
1   tablespoon (18 grams) vanilla bean paste
¼   teaspoon (1 gram) almond extract
2   cups (250 grams) all-purpose flour
⅔   cup (60 grams) rainbow sprinkles*
1½   teaspoons (7.5 grams) baking powder
1   teaspoon (3 grams) kosher salt
¼   teaspoon (1.25 grams) baking soda
1¼   cups (150 grams) confectioners' sugar
2   tablespoons (30 grams) heavy whipping cream
1   teaspoon (4 grams) vanilla extract
3   tablespoons (60 grams) strawberry fruit spread*

1. Preheat oven to 350°F (180°C).
2. In the bowl of a stand mixer fitted with the whisk attachment, beat granulated sugar and eggs at medium-high speed until pale and thick, 2 to 3 minutes. With mixer on medium speed, slowly add oil, beating until combined. Add milk, sour cream, vanilla bean paste, and almond extract; beat at medium-low speed until just combined.
3. In a medium bowl, whisk together flour, sprinkles, baking powder, salt, and baking soda. With mixer on low speed, gradually add flour mixture to sugar mixture, beating until just combined.
4. Spray a 10-cup Bundt pan with baking spray with flour. Pour batter into prepared pan. Firmly tap pan on a kitchen towel-lined counter a few times to settle batter and release any air bubbles.
5. Bake until a wooden pick inserted near center comes out clean and an instant-read thermometer inserted near center registers 205°F (96°C), 40 to 45 minutes. Using a knife or offset spatula, loosen cake from sides and center of pan. Let cool in pan for 10 minutes. Invert cake onto a wire rack, and let cool completely.
6. In a small bowl, whisk together confectioners' sugar, cream, and vanilla. Whisk in fruit spread. Spoon onto cooled cake, letting glaze drip down sides. Store in an airtight container for up to 3 days.

We used quins, sometimes called sequins or confetti sprinkles, and Bonne Maman Strawberry Fruit Spread.

CELEBRATION CAKE

Makes 1 (6-cup) cake

This small cake will bring delight to any occasion. The soft and airy crumb is studded with sprinkles and mixed with sweet strawberry preserves, making it a cake worthy of its own celebration.

¾	cup (150 grams) granulated sugar
1	large egg (50 grams), room temperature
⅓	cup (75 grams) vegetable oil
⅓	cup (80 grams) whole milk, room temperature
1	tablespoon (15 grams) sour cream, room temperature
2	teaspoons (12 grams) vanilla bean paste
⅛	teaspoon almond extract
1⅓	cups (167 grams) all-purpose flour
⅓	cup (45 grams) rainbow sprinkles*
1	teaspoon (5 grams) baking powder
½	teaspoon (1.5 grams) kosher salt
¼	teaspoon (1.25 grams) baking soda
1	cup (120 grams) confectioners' sugar
3	tablespoons (60 grams) seedless strawberry preserves*
1	tablespoon (14 grams) unsalted butter, melted

1. Preheat oven to 350°F (180°C).

2. In the bowl of a stand mixer fitted with the whisk attachment, beat granulated sugar and eggs at medium-high speed until pale and thick, 1 to 2 minutes. With mixer on medium speed, slowly add oil, beating until combined. Add milk, sour cream, vanilla bean paste, and almond extract; beat at medium-low speed until just combined.

3. In a medium bowl, whisk together flour, sprinkles, baking powder, salt, and baking soda. With mixer on low speed, gradually add flour mixture to sugar mixture, beating until just combined.

4. Spray a Nordic Ware 6-Cup Charlotte Cake Pan with baking spray with flour. Pour batter into prepared pan. Firmly tap pan on a kitchen towel-lined counter to settle batter and release any air bubbles.

5. Bake until a wooden pick inserted in center comes out clean, about 30 minutes. Let cool in pan for 10 minutes. Remove from pan, and let cool completely on a wire rack.

6. In a small bowl, whisk together confectioners' sugar and preserves until smooth. Whisk in melted butter. Immediately spread onto cooled cake. Store in an airtight container for up to 3 days.

*We used quins, sometimes called sequins or confetti sprinkles, and Bonne Maman Intense Strawberry Preserves.

SWEET TEA POUND CAKE

Makes 1 (15-cup) Bundt cake

Calling all iced tea lovers! We're taking your favorite cold drink and transforming it into your new favorite cake. This pound cake gets its moist texture and refreshing flavor from a syrup and cream infused with black tea. And because a glass of iced tea is always better with a slice of lemon, we topped this cake with citrus glaze.

1½ cups (340 grams) unsalted butter, softened
2¾ cups (550 grams) granulated sugar
7   large eggs (350 grams), room temperature
1½ teaspoons (6 grams) vanilla extract
3¼ cups (406 grams) all-purpose flour
1   teaspoon (3 grams) kosher salt
Tea-Infused Cream (recipe follows)
Sweet Tea Simple Syrup (recipe follows)
Lemon Glaze (recipe follows)

1. Preheat oven to 300°F (150°C).
2. In the bowl of a stand mixer fitted with the paddle attachment, beat butter and sugar at medium speed until fluffy, 6 to 7 minutes, stopping to scrape sides of bowl. Add eggs, one at a time, beating well after each addition. Stir in vanilla.
3. In a medium bowl, whisk together flour and salt. With mixer on low speed, gradually add flour mixture to butter mixture alternately with Tea-Infused Cream, beginning and ending with flour mixture, beating just until combined after each addition.
4. Spray a 15-cup Bundt pan with baking spray with flour. Spoon batter into prepared pan.
5. Bake for 1 hour. Loosely cover with foil, and bake until a wooden pick inserted near center comes out clean, 45 to 55 minutes more. Let cool in pan for 15 minutes. Invert cake onto a wire rack. Brush Sweet Tea Simple Syrup onto warm cake. Let stand for 15 minutes; brush Sweet Tea Simple Syrup onto cake again. Let cool completely.
6. Place a piece of parchment paper under wire rack. Spoon Lemon Glaze onto cooled cake before serving.

TEA-INFUSED CREAM

Makes 1 cup

1   cup (240 grams) heavy whipping cream, plus more if needed
2   family-size black tea bags* (16 grams)

1. In a small saucepan, heat cream over medium-low heat just until bubbles form around sides of pan. (Do not boil.) Remove from heat, and add tea bags. Let stand for 10 minutes. Discard tea bags, pressing against side of pan to remove any liquid. Pour into a liquid measuring cup to measure 1 cup (240 grams); add additional cream, if necessary. Let cool completely.

We used Luzianne Tea.

Note: *For a stronger Tea-Infused Cream, use 4 family-size tea bags in 1½ cups (360 grams) heavy whipping cream, ensuring sure you have 1 cup (240 grams) Tea-Infused Cream to use in Sweet Tea Pound Cake.*

SWEET TEA SIMPLE SYRUP

About 2 cups

1   cup (200 grams) granulated sugar
1   cup (240 grams) water
4   family-size black tea bags (32 grams)

1. In a small saucepan, bring sugar and 1 cup (240 grams) water to a boil over medium-high heat; cook for 1 minute. Remove from heat; add tea bags. Let stand for 10 minutes. Discard tea bags. Let cool completely before using.

LEMON GLAZE

Makes about 1 cup

1½ cups (180 grams) confectioners' sugar
3   tablespoons (45 grams) fresh lemon juice
1   tablespoon (21 grams) light corn syrup

1. In a medium bowl, whisk together all ingredients until smooth.

CREAM CHEESE POUND CAKE

Makes 1 (6-cup) cake

Brooke Bell grew up eating this pound cake, baked by her mom, and it's still one of her favorites. We worked to scale back the original amounts so it's even easier to make and enjoy any time she—and now you—wants. Packed full of Southern charm, this treat is destined to become your new favorite pound cake recipe!

¾   cup (170 grams) unsalted butter, softened
1½   cups (300 grams) granulated sugar
4   ounces (113 grams) cream cheese, room temperature
3   large eggs (150 grams), room temperature
1½   teaspoons (6 grams) vanilla extract
1½   cups (188 grams) all-purpose flour
½   teaspoon (1.5 grams) kosher salt
Confectioners' sugar, for dusting
Garnish: fresh berries

1. Preheat oven to 325°F (170°C).
2. In the bowl of a stand mixer fitted with the paddle attachment, beat butter and granulated sugar at medium speed until light and fluffy, 4 to 5 minutes, stopping to scrape sides of bowl. Add cream cheese, and beat until combined. Add eggs, one at a time, beating well after each addition. Beat in vanilla.
3. In a medium bowl, whisk together flour and salt. With mixer on low speed, gradually add flour mixture to butter mixture, beating until just combined.
4. Spray a Nordic Ware 6-Cup Charlotte Cake Pan with baking spray with flour. Spoon batter into prepared pan, leveling as needed. Firmly tap pan on a kitchen towel-lined counter to settle batter and release any air bubbles.
5. Bake until a wooden pick inserted near center comes out clean, 45 to 50 minutes. Let cool in pan for 10 minutes. Remove from pan, and let cool completely on a wire rack.
6. Dust cooled cake with confectioners' sugar as desired. Garnish with berries, if desired. Refrigerate in an airtight container for up to 3 days.

CHOCOLATE-HAZELNUT BANANA CAKE

Makes 1 (6-cup) Bundt cake

Ripe bananas and chocolate-hazelnut spread create a rich and decadently delicious pair in this bake.

1⅓ cups (167 grams) all-purpose flour
1 teaspoon (3 grams) kosher salt
¾ teaspoon (4 grams) baking powder
½ teaspoon (1 gram) ground cinnamon
¼ teaspoon (1.25 grams) baking soda
⅓ cup (66 grams) granulated sugar
3 tablespoons (42 grams) firmly packed light brown sugar
2 large eggs (100 grams), room temperature
1 cup (240 grams) mashed very ripe bananas (about 2 large bananas)
¼ cup (56 grams) vegetable oil
¼ cup (60 grams) whole buttermilk, room temperature
1 teaspoon (4 grams) vanilla extract
¾ cup (252 grams) chocolate-hazelnut spread*, divided
2 tablespoons (30 grams) heavy whipping cream
1 tablespoon (14 grams) unsalted butter

1. Preheat oven to 350°F (180°C).
2. In a medium bowl, whisk together flour, salt, baking powder, cinnamon, and baking soda.
3. In a large bowl, whisk together sugars and eggs. Add banana, oil, buttermilk, and vanilla, whisking until combined. Add flour mixture, and whisk until just combined and no dry spots remain.
4. Spoon ½ cup (168 grams) chocolate-hazelnut spread into a pastry bag, and cut a ¼-inch opening in tip.
5. Spray a Nordic Ware 6-Cup Charlotte Cake Pan with baking spray with flour. Spoon two-thirds of batter (about 1⅔ cups or 503 grams) into bottom of prepared pan, spreading to edges. Pipe hazelnut chocolate spread evenly over batter, leaving a ¼-inch border around edges. Using a wooden pick or skewer, level hazelnut chocolate spread and lightly swirl into batter. Top with remaining batter, spreading to edges. Firmly tap pan on a kitchen towel-lined counter to settle batter. Using a wooden pick or skewer, swirl batter.
6. Bake until a wooden pick inserted in center comes out with a few moist crumbs, 30 to 35 minutes. Let cool in pan for 10 minutes. Remove from pan, and let cool completely on a wire rack.
7. In a small microwave-safe bowl, combine cream, butter, and remaining ¼ cup (84 grams) chocolate-hazelnut spread. Heat on high in 30-second intervals, stirring between each, until butter is melted and hazelnut chocolate spread has softened. Whisk until combined. Spread ganache over cooled cake. Refrigerate in an airtight container for up to 3 days.

We used Bonne Maman Hazelnut Chocolate Spread.

Makes 1 (15-cup) cake

From its crisp, sugared exterior to its soft, velvety interior, our chocolate pound cake is a perfect blend of taste and texture.

CHOCOLATE CREAM CHEESE POUND CAKE

8   ounces (226 grams) cream cheese, cubed and softened
4   ounces (113 grams) 60% cacao dark chocolate, finely chopped
1¼ cups (106 grams) plus 2 teaspoons (4 grams) sifted Dutch process cocoa powder, divided
½   cup (120 grams) boiling water
1   tablespoon (13 grams) vanilla extract
1½ cups (340 grams) unsalted butter, softened
3   cups (600 grams) granulated sugar
6   large eggs (300 grams), room temperature
3   cups (375 grams) all-purpose flour*
2   teaspoons (6 grams) kosher salt
2   teaspoons (3 grams) instant espresso powder
½   teaspoon (2.5 grams) baking powder
2   tablespoons (16 grams) confectioners' sugar
Ganache (recipe follows)
Cocoa Whipped Cream (recipe follows)

1. Preheat oven to 325°F (170°C).
2. In the top of a double boiler, place cream cheese and chopped chocolate. Cook, without stirring, over simmering water until chocolate is almost melted. Gently stir until combined. Remove from heat. Add 1¼ cups (106 grams) cocoa and ½ cup (120 grams) boiling water, whisking until combined. Whisk in vanilla.
3. In the bowl of a stand mixer fitted with the paddle attachment, beat butter and granulated sugar at medium speed until fluffy, 5 to 7 minutes, stopping to scrape sides of bowl. Add eggs, one at a time, beating until well combined after each addition.
4. In a large bowl, whisk together flour, salt, espresso powder, and baking powder. With mixer on low speed, add flour mixture to butter mixture in three additions alternately with chocolate mixture, beginning and ending with flour mixture, beating just until combined after each addition and stopping to scrape sides of bowl.
5. Spray a 15-cup, straight-sided, light-colored metal tube pan with baking spray with flour. Spoon batter into prepared pan. Tap pan on a kitchen towel-lined counter a few times to release any air bubbles. Smooth top with an offset spatula.
6. Bake until a wooden pick inserted near center comes out clean, 1 hour and 20 minutes to 1½ hours, loosely covering with foil to prevent excess browning during final 15 minutes of baking. Let cool in pan for 15 minutes. Invert cake onto a wire rack; immediately turn cake so crust is top side up. Let cool completely.
7. In a small bowl, whisk together confectioners' sugar and remaining 2 teaspoons (4 grams) cocoa. Using a fine-mesh sieve, dust top of cooled cake with sugar mixture. Serve with Ganache and Cocoa Whipped Cream.

We used Bob's Red Mill Organic All-Purpose Flour.

GANACHE
Makes 3¾ cups

12 ounces (340 grams) 60% cacao dark chocolate, finely chopped
1¾ cups (420 grams) heavy whipping cream
2   tablespoons (42 grams) light corn syrup
2   tablespoons (28 grams) unsalted butter, softened
½   teaspoon (2 grams) vanilla extract

1. In a medium heatproof bowl, place chocolate.
2. In a small saucepan, heat cream and corn syrup over medium heat, stirring frequently, just until steaming. (Do not boil.) Pour hot cream mixture over chocolate; let stand for about 2 minutes. Using a silicone spatula, slowly stir small circles in center of bowl until mixture comes together and is shiny and smooth. Stir in butter and vanilla until fully combined. Serve warm or at room temperature. Refrigerate in an airtight container.

COCOA WHIPPED CREAM
Makes 3 cups

1½ cups (360 grams) cold heavy whipping cream
⅓   cup (40 grams) confectioners' sugar
2   tablespoons (10 grams) Dutch process cocoa powder

1. Refrigerate a large bowl and a whisk for 15 minutes.
2. In chilled bowl, using chilled whisk, whisk together all ingredients until soft to medium peaks form. Use immediately, or cover and refrigerate until ready to use. Best used same day.

BANANA BREAD-CREAM CHEESE POUND CAKE

Makes 1 (12-cup) Bundt cake

With a little optimization and some Southern charm, the iconic crackled top and moist texture of pound cake can be credited to one tangy and rich all-star addition: cream cheese. We elevated the cream cheese pound cake batter by layering it on top of a lightly spiced brown sugar-banana batter, creating a two-toned masterpiece. A final sprinkling of granulated sugar and cinnamon shows off the gorgeous design of the Bundt pan.

Cream cheese batter:
¾ cup (170 grams) unsalted butter, softened
4 ounces (113 grams) cream cheese, cubed and softened
1⅓ cups (267 grams) granulated sugar
3 large eggs (150 grams), room temperature
1 teaspoon (6 grams) vanilla bean paste
1½ cups (188 grams) all-purpose flour
¾ teaspoon (2.25 grams) kosher salt
¼ teaspoon (1.25 grams) baking powder

Banana batter:
¼ cup (57 grams) unsalted butter, softened
4 ounces (113 grams) cream cheese, cubed and softened
¾ cup (165 grams) firmly packed dark brown sugar
½ cup (100 grams) granulated sugar
1 large egg (50 grams), room temperature
1½ teaspoons (9 grams) vanilla bean paste
1⅔ cups (208 grams) all-purpose flour
1½ teaspoons (3 grams) ground cinnamon
1¼ teaspoons (3.75 grams) kosher salt
½ teaspoon (1 gram) ground nutmeg
¼ teaspoon (1.25 grams) baking powder
¾ cup (171 grams) mashed ripe banana (about 2 medium bananas)
½ cup (57 grams) finely chopped toasted pecans

Topping:
2 tablespoons (28 grams) unsalted butter, melted
¼ cup (50 grams) granulated sugar
¼ teaspoon ground cinnamon

1. Preheat oven to 325°F (170°C).

2. For cream cheese batter: In the bowl of a stand mixer fitted with the paddle attachment, beat butter at medium speed until smooth and creamy, about 1 minute, stopping to scrape sides of bowl. Add cream cheese, and beat until smooth and well combined, about 30 seconds, stopping to scrape sides of bowl. Reduce mixer speed to low; add granulated sugar, beating just until combined. Increase mixer speed to medium, and beat until fluffy, about 2 minutes, stopping to scrape sides of bowl. Add eggs, one at a time, beating until well combined after each addition. Beat in vanilla bean paste. (Mixture may look slightly curdled at this point, but batter will come together.)

3. In a medium bowl, whisk together flour, salt, and baking powder. With mixer on low speed, gradually add flour mixture to butter mixture, beating just until combined and stopping to scrape sides of bowl. Transfer batter to a large bowl.

4. For banana batter: Clean bowl of stand mixer and paddle attachment. Using the paddle attachment, beat butter at medium speed until smooth and creamy, 30 seconds to 1 minute, stopping to scrape sides of bowl. Add cream cheese, and beat until smooth and well combined, about 30 seconds, stopping to scrape sides of bowl. Reduce mixer speed to low; add brown sugar and granulated sugar, beating just until combined. Increase mixer speed to medium, and beat until fluffy, about 2 minutes, stopping to scrape sides of bowl. Add egg, beating until well combined. Beat in vanilla bean paste. (Mixture may look slightly curdled at this point, but batter will come together.)

5. In a medium bowl, whisk together flour, cinnamon, salt, nutmeg, and baking powder. With mixer on low speed, gradually add flour mixture to butter mixture alternately with banana, beginning and ending with flour mixture, beating just until some flour streaks remain. Beat in pecans just until combined.

6. Generously spray a 12-cup Bundt pan with baking spray with flour. Spoon banana batter into prepared pan in an even layer; gently spoon cream cheese batter onto banana batter in an even layer. Firmly tap pan on a kitchen towel-lined counter several times to settle batters and release as many air bubbles as possible.

7. Bake for 50 minutes; rotate pan, and bake until a wooden pick inserted near center comes out clean, crack on surface of cake appears mostly dry, and an instant-read thermometer inserted near center registers 208°F (98°C), 15 to 20 minutes more. Let cool in pan for 15 minutes. Carefully invert cake onto a wire rack placed over a rimmed baking sheet, and let cool completely.

8. For topping: Brush melted butter onto cooled cake.

9. In a small bowl, whisk together granulated sugar and cinnamon. Sprinkle mixture onto cake, gently pressing to adhere.

PRO TIP
Place an oven-safe wire rack directly on your oven rack to create a sturdy, crosshatched surface to help keep pan level and stable while baking.

PEAR-CRÈME FRAÎCHE POUND CAKE

Makes 1 (15-cup) Bundt cake

This Pear-Crème Fraîche Pound Cake balances the buttery richness of a classic pound cake with the delicately sweet flavors of fresh Bosc pears and the subtle tang of crème fraîche. But what truly gives this cake its signature dense but tender crumb is its use of eggs. They're the miracle ingredient that adds both richness with the yolks and a subtle balance of height and lightness with the whites. For added depth of flavor, the batter is flecked with seeds from vanilla bean paste and perfumed with the gentle flavor of almond extract. The resulting cake is wonderfully complex in both taste and texture.

1½   cups (340 grams) unsalted butter, softened
2¾   cups (550 grams) granulated sugar
6   large eggs (300 grams), room temperature
2   teaspoons (12 grams) vanilla bean paste
1½   teaspoons (6 grams) almond extract
3   cups (375 grams) all-purpose flour
1½   teaspoons (4.5 grams) kosher salt
½   teaspoon (2.5 grams) baking soda
1¼   cups (300 grams) crème fraîche, room temperature
2½   cups (400 grams) ½-inch-diced peeled ripe but firm Bosc pears (about 3 large pears)
Vanilla-Crème Fraîche Glaze (recipe follows)

1. Preheat oven to 350°F (180°C).
2. In the bowl of a stand mixer fitted with the paddle attachment, beat butter and sugar at low speed just until combined. Increase mixer speed to medium, and beat until fluffy, about 3 minutes, stopping to scrape sides of bowl. Add eggs, one at a time, beating well after each addition and stopping to scrape sides of bowl. Beat in vanilla bean paste and almond extract. (Mixture may look slightly curdled at this point, but batter will come together.)
3. In a medium bowl, whisk together flour, salt, and baking soda. With mixer on low speed, gradually add flour mixture to butter mixture alternately with crème fraîche, beginning and ending with flour mixture, beating just until combined after each addition and stopping to scrape sides of bowl. Fold in pears.
4. Generously spray a 15-cup Bundt pan with baking spray with flour. Spoon batter into prepared pan. Tap pan on counter several times to evenly spread batter and release any air bubbles. (Pan will be quite full, but batter will not overflow during baking.)

5. Bake until a wooden pick inserted near center comes out clean and an instant-read thermometer registers 205°F (96°C) to 210°F (98°C), 1 hour and 10 minutes to 1 hour and 20 minutes, rotating pan halfway through baking and loosely covering with foil to prevent excess browning, if necessary. Let cool in pan for 20 minutes. Using a small offset spatula, gently loosen cake from center and edges of pan. Invert cake onto a wire rack, and let cool completely.
6. Spoon and spread Vanilla-Crème Fraîche Glaze onto cooled cake as desired. Let stand until glaze is set, about 15 minutes.

Vanilla-Crème Fraîche Glaze

Makes about ¾ cup

1½   cups (180 grams) confectioners' sugar
3   tablespoons (45 grams) crème fraîche
1   teaspoon (6 grams) vanilla bean paste
¼   teaspoon kosher salt
5   teaspoons (25 grams) heavy whipping cream

1. In a medium bowl, whisk together confectioners' sugar, crème fraîche, vanilla bean paste, and salt. Add cream, whisking until mixture is smooth and pourable. Use immediately.

COFFEE AND CREAM MARBLED COFFEE CAKE

Makes 1 (9-inch) cake

Enriched with bittersweet chocolate and espresso, this Coffee and Cream Marbled Coffee Cake will take your morning beverage to new, delightful heights. Espresso Streusel adorns the top of this creamy, rich cake, adding a textured crunch to each bite.

1¼	cups (284 grams) unsalted butter, softened	
2¼	cups (450 grams) granulated sugar	
5	large eggs (250 grams), room temperature	
1	tablespoon (13 grams) vanilla extract	
3	cups (375 grams) all-purpose flour	
2½	teaspoons (12.5 grams) baking powder	
1	teaspoon (3 grams) kosher salt	
¾	cup (180 grams) sour cream, room temperature	
3	ounces (85 grams) 60% cacao bittersweet chocolate, melted and cooled slightly	
3	tablespoons (21 grams) instant espresso powder	

Espresso Streusel (recipe follows)

1. Preheat oven to 350°F (180°C).

2. In the bowl of a stand mixer fitted with the paddle attachment, beat butter and sugar at medium speed until fluffy, 3 to 4 minutes, stopping to scrape sides of bowl. Add eggs, one at a time, beating well after each addition. Beat in vanilla.

3. In a medium bowl, whisk together flour, baking powder, and salt. With mixer on low speed, add flour mixture to butter mixture in three additions alternately with sour cream, beginning and ending with flour mixture, beating just until combined after each addition. Divide batter in half (about 3 cups or 780 grams each).

4. In a small bowl, stir together melted chocolate and espresso powder until espresso fully dissolves; stir into one portion of batter until combined. Leave remaining portion of batter as is.

5. Using 2 (1½-tablespoon) spring-loaded scoops, scoop batters in an alternating pattern into bottom of a 9-inch nonstick tube pan. (See Note.) Firmly tap pan on a kitchen towel-lined counter 2 or 3 times to help level batter and fill pan. Create another layer with alternating cake batters. Tap pan again. Scoop remaining batter randomly on top. Using a butter knife, swirl batters together in a figure eight motion. Tap pan again to help level batter and fill in any gaps. Sprinkle Espresso Streusel on top, making sure to break up any large chunks.

6. Bake until a wooden pick inserted in center comes out clean, about 1 hour and 5 minutes, loosely covering with foil to prevent excess browning, if necessary. Let cool in pan for 20 minutes. Remove from pan. Best served warm.

Note: *Using a regular tube pan will work; you just need to spray it first with baking spray with flour. The bake time remains the same, but the edges will be crispy and not as pretty.*

ESPRESSO STREUSEL

Makes about 1 cup

⅔	cup (83 grams) all-purpose flour	
⅓	cup (67 grams) granulated sugar	
1	tablespoon (7 grams) instant espresso powder	
¼	teaspoon kosher salt	
¼	cup (57 grams) cold unsalted butter, cubed	

1. In a medium bowl, whisk together flour, sugar, espresso powder, and salt. Using a pastry blender or 2 forks, cut in cold butter until combined and mixture is crumbly. Mix with your hands until completely combined and no more butter lumps remain. (Mixture should resemble wet sand.) Freeze until ready to use.

LEMON POUND CAKE

Makes 1 (10-cup) Bundt cake

This bright citrus Bundt cake is the perfect dessert for any lemon lover. Packed with sunny lemon zest and tangy sour cream, each bite pops with lemony goodness. Cover with a beautiful glaze to finish off this summer showstopper.

1   cup (227 grams) unsalted butter, softened
2⅔   cups (533 grams) granulated sugar
4   large eggs (200 grams), room temperature
1   tablespoon (7 grams) tightly packed lemon zest
2   teaspoons (8 grams) vanilla extract
2⅓   cups (292 grams) all-purpose flour
1¼   teaspoons (3.75 grams) kosher salt
½   teaspoon (2.5 grams) baking soda
1   cup (240 grams) sour cream, room temperature
Fresh Lemon Glaze (recipe follows)

1. Preheat oven to 325°F (170°C).
2. In the bowl of a stand mixer fitted with the paddle attachment, beat butter and sugar with a mixer at medium speed until fluffy, 5 to 6 minutes, stopping to scrape sides of bowl. Add eggs, one at a time, beating well after each addition. Beat in lemon zest and vanilla.
3. In a medium bowl, whisk together flour, salt, and baking soda. With mixer on low speed, gradually add flour mixture to butter mixture alternately with sour cream, beginning and ending with flour mixture, beating just until combined after each addition. (Batter will be thick.)
4. Spray a 10-cup Bundt pan with baking spray with flour. Spoon batter into prepared pan. Tap pan on a kitchen towel-lined counter several times to settle batter and release any air bubbles.
5. Bake until a wooden pick inserted near center comes out clean, 1 hour and 5 minutes to 1 hour and 15 minutes. Let cool in pan for 10 minutes. Invert cake onto a wire rack, and let cool completely. Drizzle Fresh Lemon Glaze onto cooled cake. Cover and refrigerate for up to 3 days.

FRESH LEMON GLAZE
Makes about ½ cup

1½   cups (180 grams) confectioners' sugar
6 to 7 teaspoons (30 to 35 grams) fresh lemon juice
1   teaspoon (2 grams) lightly packed lemon zest

1. In a small bowl, whisk together all ingredients until smooth. Use immediately.

BUTTER PECAN POUND CAKE

Makes 1 (15-cup) Bundt cake

A buttery bake packed with nutty pecans, this cake is the definition of comfort. Sour cream in the batter gives it an extra-tender crumb while brown sugar brings out the warmth and richness of the pecans. We used both finely chopped pecans and pecan pieces to ensure that each bite of cake held a nutty morsel, big or small.

1½	cups (340 grams) unsalted butter, softened
1⅔	cups (333 grams) granulated sugar
1	cup (220 grams) firmly packed dark brown sugar
7	large eggs (350 grams)
1½	teaspoons (6 grams) vanilla extract
3¼	cups (406 grams) all-purpose flour
1	teaspoon (3 grams) kosher salt
1	cup (240 grams) sour cream
1¼	cups (141 grams) pecan pieces, divided
½	cup (57 grams) plus 2 tablespoons (14 grams) finely chopped pecans, divided

White Icing (recipe follows)

1. Preheat oven to 300°F (150°C).
2. In the bowl of a stand mixer fitted with the paddle attachment, beat butter and sugars at medium speed until fluffy, 6 to 7 minutes, stopping to scrape sides of bowl. Add eggs, one at a time, beating well after each addition. Stir in vanilla.
3. In a medium bowl, sift together flour and salt. With mixer on low speed, gradually add flour mixture to butter mixture alternately with sour cream, beginning and ending with flour mixture, beating just until combined after each addition. Add 1 cup (113 grams) pecan pieces and ½ cup (57 grams) chopped pecans, and beat until evenly distributed.
4. Spray a 15-cup Bundt pan with baking spray with flour. Spoon batter into prepared pan. Tap pan on a kitchen towel-lined counter 5 to 6 times to release air bubbles. Smooth top.
5. Bake until a wooden pick inserted near center comes out clean, 1 hour and 35 minutes to 1 hour and 45 minutes. Let cool in pan for 20 minutes. Invert cake onto a wire rack, and let cool completely. Spoon White Icing onto cooled cake.
6. In a small bowl, combine remaining ¼ cup (28 grams) pecan pieces and remaining 2 tablespoons (14 grams) chopped pecans. Sprinkle on top of icing. Store in an airtight container for up to 3 days.

WHITE ICING
Makes about 1 cup

1¼	cups (150 grams) confectioners' sugar
4½	tablespoons (67.5 grams) heavy whipping cream
1	tablespoon (21 grams) light corn syrup

1. In a medium bowl, whisk together all ingredients until smooth.

CHOCOLATE
DECADENCE

CHOCOLATE LOVERS, REJOICE!
WE HAVE A BAKE FOR EVERY CHOCOHOLIC.

CHOCOLATE-SWIRLED PEANUT BUTTER-BANANA BUNDT CAKE

Makes 1 (10-cup) Bundt cake

This oh-so-satisfying cake marries a moist banana and peanut butter batter with melted chocolate and gorgeously gilded with even more chocolate decadence.

1   cup (200 grams) granulated sugar
¾   cup (168 grams) neutral oil
⅔   cup (185 grams) mashed very ripe banana (about 2 medium bananas)
½   cup (110 grams) firmly packed light brown sugar
½   cup (128 grams) creamy peanut butter
2   large eggs (100 grams), room temperature
2   teaspoons (8 grams) vanilla extract
1   cup (240 grams) whole buttermilk, room temperature
2½   cups (313 grams) all-purpose flour
2   teaspoons (10 grams) baking powder
1   teaspoon (3 grams) kosher salt
1   ounce (28 grams) 60% to 70% cacao bittersweet chocolate, finely chopped
Chocolate Glaze (recipe follows)

1. Preheat oven to 325°F (170°C).
2. In a large bowl, whisk together granulated sugar, oil, banana, brown sugar, and peanut butter until well combined, about 1 minute. Add eggs and vanilla; whisk until well combined. Whisk in buttermilk.
3. In a medium bowl, whisk together flour, baking powder, and salt. Sift flour mixture over sugar mixture. Gently stir until all dry ingredients are moistened. (Do not overmix; batter will not be smooth.)
4. In a medium microwave-safe bowl, heat chocolate on high in 30-seconds intervals, stirring between each, until melted and smooth. Stir ¾ cup (217 grams) batter into melted chocolate just until combined.

5. Spray a 10-cup Bundt pan with baking spray with flour. Spoon 2 cups (586 grams) plain batter into prepared pan. Firmly tap pan on a kitchen towel-lined counter 4 to 5 times to settle batter and release any air bubbles. Using the back of a small spoon, create a trench in batter in pan. Spoon dollops of chocolate and plain batters alternately into trench, taking care that chocolate batter does not touch sides of pan. Firmly tap pan on kitchen towel-lined counter 2 to 3 times to settle batter. Repeat alternating dollops of batters until all chocolate batter is used. Using a butter knife, swirl batters. Gently spread remaining plain batter on top. Firmly tap pan on kitchen towel-lined counter once to settle batter.
6. Bake until golden brown, a wooden pick inserted near center comes out clean, and an instant-read thermometer inserted near center registers 205°F (96°C), about 1 hour and 5 minutes. Let cool in pan for 15 minutes. Invert cake onto a wire rack, and let cool completely.
7. Spoon Chocolate Glaze onto cooled cake; tap wire rack on counter to smooth and settle glaze on cake.

CHOCOLATE GLAZE
Makes about ¾ cup

4   ounces (113 grams) 60% to 70% cacao bittersweet chocolate, finely chopped
½   cup (120 grams) heavy whipping cream
1   tablespoon (21 grams) light corn syrup

1. In a small bowl, place chocolate.
2. In a small saucepan, heat cream and corn syrup over medium heat, stirring frequently, until steaming. (Do not boil.) Immediately pour onto chocolate; let stand for 5 minutes. Starting in center of bowl, slowly stir mixture with a rubber spatula until well combined. Use immediately.

BROWNIE BUNDT CAKE

Makes 1 (12-cup) Bundt cake

Dark yet smooth, Dutch process cocoa powder gives this Brownie Bundt Cake extra-chocolaty depth of flavor while oil and sour cream boost the moist and fudgy texture. A final dusting of edible gold glitter and it's officially an occasion for celebration.

¾ cup (170 grams) unsalted butter, cubed
7 ounces (198 grams) 60% cacao bittersweet chocolate, finely chopped and divided
1 cup (85 grams) sifted Dutch process cocoa powder
½ cup (120 grams) boiling water (see PRO TIPS)
2 teaspoons (3 grams) instant espresso powder
1¼ cups (250 grams) granulated sugar
⅔ cup (147 grams) firmly packed dark brown sugar
⅓ cup (75 grams) canola oil
5 large eggs (250 grams), room temperature
½ cup (120 grams) sour cream, room temperature
1 tablespoon (13 grams) vanilla extract
2 cups (250 grams) all-purpose flour
1¾ teaspoons (5.25 grams) kosher salt
Garnish: edible gold glitter spray

1. Preheat oven to 325°F (170°C).
2. In the top of a double boiler, combine butter and 4 ounces (113 grams) chocolate. Cook over simmering water, stirring occasionally, until melted and smooth. Remove from heat; whisk in cocoa, ½ cup (120 grams) boiling water, and espresso powder until smooth and well combined. Whisk in sugars.
3. In a large bowl, whisk together chocolate mixture and oil. Gradually whisk in eggs until combined. Whisk in sour cream and vanilla.
4. In a medium bowl, whisk together flour and salt. Gradually fold flour mixture into chocolate mixture just until a few bits of flour remain. Fold in remaining 3 ounces (85 grams) chocolate.
5. Spray a 12-cup Bundt pan with baking spray with flour. Pour batter into prepared pan. Tap pan on a kitchen towel-lined counter several times to release any air bubbles.
6. Bake until a wooden pick inserted near center comes out clean, 1 hour to 1 hour and 10 minutes. Let cool in pan for 10 minutes. Invert cake onto a wire rack, and let cool completely. Garnish with edible glitter spray, if desired.

PRO TIPS

For best accuracy, be sure to use already-boiling water to measure out what is needed in this recipe.

Place an oven-safe wire rack directly on your oven rack to create a sturdy, crosshatched surface to help keep pan level and stable while baking.

CHOCOLATE-CITRUS CHOCOFLAN

Makes 1 (10-cup) Bundt cake

*Aptly nicknamed pastel imposible in Spanish, or "impossible cake,"
the chocoflan is originally from Mexico and is one of its most prized
variations of flan. In this recipe, a spike of orange zest and the addition
of a little cream cheese in the flan layer make for a lusciously smooth,
slightly tart, and citrusy flan.*

Flan:

½   (12-ounce) can (184 grams) evaporated milk (about ¾ cup)
¾   (14-ounce) can (190 grams) sweetened condensed milk (about ⅔ cup)
2   large eggs (100 grams), room temperature
2   ounces (57 grams) cream cheese, room temperature
¾   teaspoon (3 grams) vanilla extract
¼   teaspoon kosher salt
¼   teaspoon (1 gram) tightly packed orange zest

Batter:

1¼ cups (156 grams) all-purpose flour
¾   cup (150 grams) granulated sugar
½   cup (43 grams) unsweetened cocoa powder
⅓   cup (73 grams) firmly packed light brown sugar
2   teaspoons (2 grams) instant espresso powder
¾   teaspoon (3.75 grams) baking soda
¼   teaspoon (1.25 grams) baking powder
¾   teaspoon (2.25 grams) kosher salt
⅔   cup (160 grams) sour cream, room temperature
¼   cup (56 grams) vegetable oil
2   large eggs (100 grams), room temperature
2   tablespoons (30 grams) water, room temperature
1   tablespoon (15 grams) coffee liqueur*
1   teaspoon (4 grams) vanilla extract

Topping:

½   cup (140 grams) dulce de leche
4   teaspoons (20 grams) fresh orange juice
¼   teaspoon kosher salt
½   teaspoon (2.5 grams) coffee liqueur

1. Preheat oven to 350°F (180°C).
2. For flan: In the container of a blender, process milks, eggs,
cream cheese, vanilla, salt, and orange zest until smooth and well
combined, about 30 seconds. Strain through a fine-mesh sieve into
a large bowl or glass measuring cup.
3. For batter: In a medium bowl, sift together flour, granulated
sugar, cocoa, brown sugar, espresso powder, baking soda, and baking
powder, pressing through any solids with a silicone spatula. Whisk
in salt.
4. In a large bowl, whisk together sour cream, oil, eggs,
2 tablespoons (30 grams) room temperature water, liqueur, and
vanilla. Gradually stir in flour mixture just until combined.
5. Spray a 10-cup Bundt pan with baking spray with flour. Spoon
batter into prepared pan. Tap pan on a kitchen towel-lined counter
a few times to settle batter and release any air bubbles. Place Bundt
pan in a 13x9-inch baking pan.
6. Hold a regular spoon about 1 inch above batter in pan; pour flan
mixture into spoon, letting it overflow gently and evenly onto batter.
(It's OK if batter and flan mixture mix just slightly). Loosely cover
Bundt pan with a greased sheet of foil. Carefully place baking pan in
oven; add enough hot water to come 1 inch up sides of Bundt pan.
7. Bake until cake is firm to the touch, a wooden pick inserted near
center comes out clean, and an instant-read thermometer inserted
near center registers 194°F (90°C) to 200°F (93°C), 1 hour and
45 minutes to 2 hours and 10 minutes. (Do not check cake too
early or often.) Remove Bundt pan from baking pan; uncover and
let cake cool in Bundt pan on a wire rack for 1 hour. Loosely cover
with foil, and refrigerate overnight.
8. To serve, let stand at room temperature for 45 minutes. Place
Bundt pan in a 13x9-inch baking pan; fill with enough very hot water
to come 1 inch up sides of Bundt pan. Let stand for 5 minutes. Using
a small offset spatula, gently loosen center and edges of cake, only
going about halfway down pan. Loosen 3 to 4 scalloped edges by
reaching offset spatula almost all the way down and gently pushing
inward to help loosen flan portion. (The aim is to break the seal and
allow the cake to release; it's OK to have minor dings in the flan
portion.) Invert pan onto a cake plate. Shake, tap, and jiggle pan
vigorously until you feel cake release; continue to loosen edges as
needed. Remove pan.
9. For topping: In a small microwave-safe bowl, heat dulce de
leche, orange juice, and salt on high in 10-second intervals, stirring
between each, until smooth and pourable. Stir in liqueur. Drizzle
onto flan; serve immediately.

We used Kahlúa.

bake it a BUNDTLETTE

CHOCOLATE-CITRUS CHOCOFLAN BUNDTLETTES

Makes 6 Bundtlettes

Flan:
⅓ cup (80 grams) evaporated milk
⅓ cup (97.5 grams) sweetened condensed milk
1 large egg (50 grams), room temperature
1 ounce (28 grams) cream cheese, room temperature
¼ teaspoon (1 gram) vanilla extract
⅛ teaspoon kosher salt
⅛ teaspoon packed orange zest

Batter:
⅔ cup (83 grams) all-purpose flour
6 tablespoons (72 grams) granulated sugar
¼ cup (21 grams) unsweetened cocoa powder
2½ tablespoons (35 grams) firmly packed light brown sugar
1 teaspoon (1 gram) instant espresso powder
¼ teaspoon (1.25 grams) baking soda
⅛ teaspoon baking powder
¼ teaspoon kosher salt
⅓ cup (80 grams) sour cream, room temperature
1 large egg (50 grams), room temperature
2 tablespoons (28 grams) vegetable oil
1 tablespoon (15 grams) water, room temperature
1½ teaspoons (7.5 grams) coffee liqueur*
½ teaspoon (2 grams) vanilla extract

Topping:
½ cup (140 grams) dulce de leche
4 teaspoons (20 grams) fresh orange juice
¼ teaspoon kosher salt
½ teaspoon (2.5 grams) coffee liqueur

1. Preheat oven to 350°F (180°C).
2. For flan: In the container of a blender, process milks, egg, cream cheese, vanilla, salt, and orange zest until smooth and well combined, about 30 seconds. Strain through a fine-mesh sieve into a medium bowl or glass measuring cup.

3. For batter: In a medium bowl, sift together flour, granulated sugar, cocoa, brown sugar, espresso powder, baking soda, and baking powder, pressing through any solids with a silicone spatula. Whisk in salt.
4. In a large bowl, whisk together sour cream, egg, oil, 1 tablespoon (15 grams) room temperature water, liqueur, and vanilla. Gradually stir in flour mixture just until combined.
5. Spray a 5-cup Bundtlette pan (see Note) with baking spray with flour. Divide batter among prepared wells. Tap pan on a kitchen towel-lined counter a few times to settle batter and release any air bubbles. Gently pour enough flan mixture over batter in each well to come up about ½ inch from top edge. (It's OK if batter and flan mixture mix just slightly). Loosely cover pan with a greased sheet of foil.
6. Place a 13x9-inch baking pan in oven; pour hot water to a depth of 1½ to 1¾ inches. Place Bundtlette pan in prepared baking pan.
7. Bake until cakes are firm to the touch, a wooden pick inserted near center comes out clean, and an instant-read thermometer inserted near center registers 194°F (90°C) to 200°F (93°C), 50 minutes to 1 hour. (Do not check cakes too early or often.) Remove Bundtlette pan from baking pan; uncover and let cakes cool in Bundtlette pan on a wire rack for 1 hour. Loosely cover with foil, and refrigerate overnight.
8. To serve, let stand at room temperature for 45 minutes.
9. In a 13x9-inch baking pan, pour very hot water to a depth of 1½ to 1¾ inches; place Bundtlette pan in hot water bath. Let stand for 5 minutes. Using a small offset spatula, gently loosen centers and edges of Bundtlettes, only going about halfway down pan. On one edge, reach all the way down with offset spatula, and gently push inward to help loosen flan portion. (The aim is to break the seal and allow the cake to release; it's OK to have minor dings in the flan portion.) Invert Bundtlette pan onto a serving plate. Shake, tap, and jiggle pan vigorously until you feel cakes release.
10. For topping: In a small microwave-safe bowl, heat dulce de leche, orange juice, and salt on high in 10-second intervals, stirring between each, until smooth and pourable. Stir in liqueur. Drizzle onto flan; serve immediately.

*We used Kahlúa.

Note: A more open, less intricately designed Bundtlette pan is ideal for these cakes.

With a delicate flan layer involved in this cake, using a more open, less intricately designed pan is ideal. The Elegant Party Bundt Pan's rounded, scalloped sides easily release this Bundt with an eye-catching shape.

A crown of dulce de leche glaze acts as a nod to flan's classic caramel component while also highlighting the Elegant Party Bundt Pan's lovely grooves.

To create distinct layers, pour the flan mixture into the bowl of a regular spoon held 1 inch over the batter in the pan. The flan mixture will overflow gently and evenly onto the batter; the two will almost magically swap places while baking, making for this mesmerizing two-tone Bundt.

As with traditional flans, you need to break a suction-like seal to allow this cake to release. Using a small offset spatula, reach almost all the way into the pan along one scalloped edge and gently push inward to loosen. (It's OK to have minor dings in the flan portion.) Once the Bundt is inverted onto a cake plate, shake, tap, and jiggle the pan vigorously until the cake lets go.

TIRAMISÙ CAKE

Makes 1 (6-cup) cake

You can have your cake and your tiramisù, too! This two-toned cake perfectly blends vanilla batter with a deep, rich chocolaty espresso batter in complete harmony. All that's left after baking is a topping of creamy mascarpone and a sweet dusting of cocoa, and you have all the elements of this beloved dessert, down to the scalloped ladyfinger-like edges courtesy of the Nordic Ware Charlotte Cake Pan.

⅔ cup (150 grams) unsalted butter, softened
1 cup (200 grams) granulated sugar
2 large eggs (100 grams), room temperature
1 teaspoon (4 grams) vanilla extract
1¼ cups (156 grams) all-purpose flour
1¼ teaspoons (6.25 grams) baking powder
¾ teaspoon (2.25 grams) kosher salt
⅓ cup (80 grams) full-fat Greek yogurt, room temperature
1 tablespoon (15 grams) whole milk
1 ounce (28 grams) 60% cacao bittersweet chocolate, melted and cooled slightly
1 tablespoon (4 grams) instant espresso powder
Whipped Mascarpone (recipe follows)
Unsweetened cocoa powder, for sifting

1. Preheat oven to 350°F (180°C).
2. In the bowl of a stand mixer fitted with the paddle attachment, beat butter and sugar at medium speed until fluffy, 3 to 4 minutes, stopping to scrape sides of bowl. Add eggs, one at a time, beating well after each addition. Beat in vanilla.
3. In a medium bowl, whisk together flour, baking powder, and salt. In a small bowl, whisk together yogurt and milk until combined. With mixer on low speed, add flour mixture to butter mixture in three additions alternately with yogurt mixture, beginning and ending with flour mixture, beating just until combined after each addition.
4. In another medium bowl, whisk together melted chocolate and espresso powder until espresso fully dissolves. Stir half of batter in chocolate mixture.
5. Spray a Nordic Ware 6-Cup Charlotte Cake Pan with baking spray with flour. Spoon plain and chocolate batters in an alternating pattern into prepared pan. Firmly tap pan on a kitchen towel-lined counter to settle batter. Using a wooden pick or skewer, swirl batters.
6. Bake until a wooden pick inserted in center comes out clean, 25 to 30 minutes. Let cool in pan for 10 minutes. Remove from pan, and let cool completely on a wire rack.
7. Spread Whipped Mascarpone onto cake and sift with cocoa powder just before serving. Refrigerate in an airtight container for up to 3 days.

WHIPPED MASCARPONE
Makes about 2 cups

½ cup (113 grams) mascarpone cheese, room temperature
¼ cup (30 grams) confectioners' sugar
½ teaspoon (2 grams) vanilla extract
¼ teaspoon kosher salt
¾ cup (180 grams) cold heavy whipping cream

1. In the bowl of a stand mixer fitted with the whisk attachment, beat mascarpone, confectioners' sugar, vanilla, and salt at medium speed until smooth and well combined; scrape sides of bowl. With mixer on medium speed, slowly add cold cream, beating until fully combined. Increase mixer speed to medium-high, and beat until soft peaks form, stopping to scrape sides of bowl. Cover and refrigerate for up to 2 hours before using.

COOKIES AND MILK BUNDT CAKE

Makes 1 (10-cup) Bundt cake

There are few desserts more iconic than the chocolate chip cookie—and some of us can't resist the urge to sample the dough before it's baked. With each bite of cake that's made tender with whole milk and crème fraîche, you'll encounter a tunnel of cookie dough, rich with brown sugar and speckled with vanilla bean seeds.

1	cup (227 grams) unsalted butter, softened
1½	cups (330 grams) firmly packed dark brown sugar
½	cup (100 grams) granulated sugar
4	large eggs (200 grams), room temperature
2	teaspoons (12 grams) vanilla bean paste
2⅔	cups (333 grams) all-purpose flour
1¼	teaspoons (3.75 grams) kosher salt
¼	teaspoon (1.25 grams) baking soda
⅔	cup (160 grams) crème fraîche, room temperature
¼	cup (60 grams) whole milk, room temperature
8	ounces (226 grams) 60% cacao bittersweet chocolate, chopped into ¼-inch pieces (about 1⅓ cups)

Cookie Dough Filling (recipe follows)
Creamy Milk Glaze (recipe follows)
Garnish: chopped chocolate chip cookies

1. Preheat oven to 325°F (170°C).
2. In the bowl of a stand mixer fitted with the paddle attachment, beat butter and sugars at medium-low speed just until combined. Increase mixer speed to medium, and beat until fluffy, 3 to 4 minutes, stopping to scrape sides of bowl. Add eggs, one at a time, beating well after each addition. Beat in vanilla bean paste.
3. In a medium bowl, whisk together flour, salt, and baking soda. In a small bowl, whisk together crème fraîche and milk. With mixer on low speed, gradually add flour mixture to butter mixture alternately with crème fraîche mixture, beginning and ending with flour mixture, beating just until combined after each addition and stopping to scrape sides of bowl. Fold in chocolate.
4. Spray a 10-cup Bundt pan with baking spray with flour. Spoon batter into prepared pan. Firmly tap pan on a kitchen towel-lined counter several times to settle batter and release any air bubbles.
5. Bake for 50 minutes. Rotate pan, and loosely cover with foil to prevent excess browning, if necessary. Bake until a wooden pick

inserted near center comes out clean, 12 to 18 minutes more. Let cool in pan for 15 minutes. Invert pan onto a wire rack; tap rack with pan on counter a few times to help loosen cake. Remove pan, and let cake cool completely on wire rack.
6. On a cutting board, place cooled cake upside down. Using a small knife, cut a 1½-inch-wide trench in bottom of cake, leaving a ¾-inch border around all edges. Using a small spoon, remove top layer (¼ to ½ inch thick) from trench, reserving removed cake pieces; set aside. Repeat until you have a 1¼- to 1½-inch-deep trench, keeping large pieces intact.
7. Spoon Cookie Dough Filling into trench, smoothing into an even layer; cover with reserved top layer, trimming pieces to fit and using extra cake pieces to patch any holes, if necessary. Place a serving plate on cake, and turn so cake is right side up.
8. Drizzle Creamy Milk Glaze onto cake; garnish with cookies, if desired.

COOKIE DOUGH FILLING
Makes about 1 cup

⅓	cup (76 grams) unsalted butter, softened
½	cup (110 grams) firmly packed dark brown sugar
1	teaspoon (6 grams) vanilla bean paste
½	cup (48 grams) superfine blanched almond flour
¼	teaspoon kosher salt
2	ounces (57 grams) 60% cacao bittersweet chocolate, finely chopped (about ⅓ cup)

1. In the bowl of a stand mixer fitted with the paddle attachment, beat butter and brown sugar at medium speed until fluffy, 2 to 3 minutes, stopping to scrape sides of bowl. Beat in vanilla bean paste.
2. In a small bowl, whisk together flour and salt. Add flour mixture to butter mixture; beat at low speed just until combined. Fold in chocolate. Use immediately.

CREAMY MILK GLAZE
Makes about ¾ cup

1¾	cups (210 grams) confectioners' sugar
2	tablespoons (30 grams) whole milk
1½	tablespoons (22.5 grams) crème fraîche
¼	teaspoon kosher salt

1. In a medium bowl, whisk together all ingredients until smooth and well combined. Use immediately.

bake it a **BUNDT**LETTE

COOKIES AND MILK BUNDTLETTES

Makes 6 Bundtlettes

½   cup (113 grams) unsalted butter, softened
¾   cup (165 grams) firmly packed dark brown sugar
¼   cup (50 grams) granulated sugar
2   large eggs (100 grams), room temperature
1   teaspoon (6 grams) vanilla bean paste
1⅓ cups (167 grams) all-purpose flour
½   teaspoon (1.5 grams) kosher salt
⅛   teaspoon baking soda
⅓   cup (80 grams) crème fraîche, room temperature
2   tablespoons (30 grams) whole milk, room temperature
4   ounces (113 grams) 60% cacao bittersweet chocolate, chopped into ¼-inch pieces (about ⅔ cup)
Bundtlette Cookie Dough Filling (recipe follows)
Bundtlette Creamy Milk Glaze (recipe follows)
Garnish: chopped chocolate chip cookies

1. Preheat oven to 325°F (170°C).
2. In the bowl of a stand mixer fitted with the paddle attachment, beat butter and sugars at medium-low speed just until combined. Increase mixer speed to medium, and beat until fluffy, 3 to 4 minutes, stopping to scrape sides of bowl. Add eggs, one at a time, beating well after each addition. Beat in vanilla bean paste.
3. In a medium bowl, whisk together flour, salt, and baking soda. In a small bowl, whisk together crème fraîche and milk. With mixer on low speed, gradually add flour mixture to butter mixture alternately with crème fraîche mixture, beginning and ending with flour mixture, beating just until combined after each addition. Fold in chocolate.
4. Spray a 4- to 5-cup Bundtlette pan with baking spray with flour. (See Note.) Divide batter among wells. Tap pan on a kitchen towel-lined counter several times to settle batter and release any air bubbles.
5. Bake until a wooden pick inserted near center comes out clean, 14 to 18 minutes. Let cool in pan for 15 minutes. Invert Bundtlettes onto a wire rack, and let cool completely.
6. On a cutting board, place cooled Bundtlettes upside down. Using a small knife, cut a ½- to ¾-inch-wide trench in bottom of each Bundtlette, leaving ¼-inch border around all edges. Using a small spoon, remove top layer (¼ to ½ inch thick) from trench, reserving removed cake pieces; set aside. Repeat until you have a ½- to ¾-inch-deep trench, keeping large pieces intact.

7. Spoon Bundtlette Cookie Dough Filling into trenches, smoothing into an even layer; cover with reserved top layers, trimming pieces to fit and using extra cake pieces to patch any holes, if necessary. Place Bundtlettes, right side up, on a serving platter.
8. Drizzle Bundtlette Creamy Milk Glaze onto cakes; garnish with cookies, if desired.

Note: *This recipe fits a 4- to 5-cup-capacity Bundtlette pan. For Bundtlette pans with smaller capacities, fill wells only two-thirds to three-fourths full.*

Bundtlette Cookie Dough Filling
Makes about ½ cup

3   tablespoons (42 grams) unsalted butter, softened
¼   cup (55 grams) firmly packed dark brown sugar
½   teaspoon (3 grams) vanilla bean paste
¼   cup (24 grams) superfine blanched almond flour
⅛   teaspoon kosher salt
1   ounce (28 grams) 60% cacao bittersweet chocolate, finely chopped (about 2½ tablespoons)

1. In a medium bowl, stir together butter and brown sugar until fluffy and well combined. Stir in vanilla bean paste.
2. In a small bowl, whisk together flour and salt. Add flour mixture to butter mixture; stir just until combined. Fold in chocolate. Use immediately.

Bundtlette Creamy Milk Glaze
Makes about ¾ cup

1¾ cups (210 grams) confectioners' sugar
2   tablespoons (30 grams) whole milk
1½ tablespoons (22.5 grams) crème fraîche
¼   teaspoon kosher salt

1. In a medium bowl, whisk together all ingredients until smooth. Use immediately.

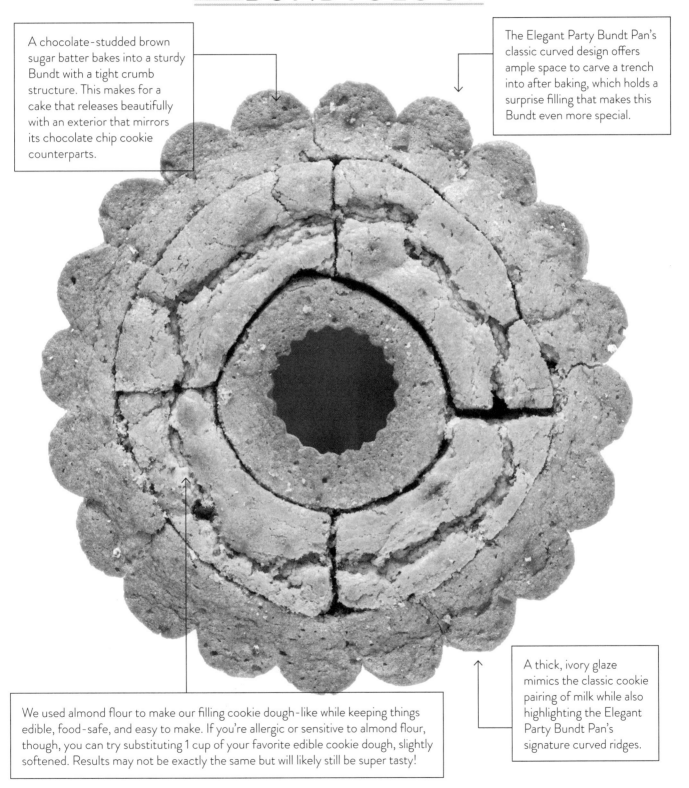

A chocolate-studded brown sugar batter bakes into a sturdy Bundt with a tight crumb structure. This makes for a cake that releases beautifully with an exterior that mirrors its chocolate chip cookie counterparts.

The Elegant Party Bundt Pan's classic curved design offers ample space to carve a trench into after baking, which holds a surprise filling that makes this Bundt even more special.

We used almond flour to make our filling cookie dough-like while keeping things edible, food-safe, and easy to make. If you're allergic or sensitive to almond flour, though, you can try substituting 1 cup of your favorite edible cookie dough, slightly softened. Results may not be exactly the same but will likely still be super tasty!

A thick, ivory glaze mimics the classic cookie pairing of milk while also highlighting the Elegant Party Bundt Pan's signature curved ridges.

CHURRO POUND CAKE WITH CHOCOLATE SAUCE

Makes 1 (15-cup) Bundt cake

Filled with sugar and warm spices, this recipe is a churro in cake form! Serve with our decadent Chocolate Sauce for a luxurious finish.

1½ cups (340 grams) unsalted butter, softened
2 cups (440 grams) plus 2 tablespoons (28 grams) firmly packed light brown sugar, divided
5 large eggs (250 grams), room temperature
2 teaspoons (8 grams) vanilla extract
3 cups (375 grams) all-purpose flour
2 teaspoons (4 grams) ground cinnamon, divided
1 teaspoon (5 grams) baking powder
1 teaspoon (3 grams) kosher salt
½ teaspoon (1 gram) ground nutmeg
1 cup (240 grams) sour cream, room temperature
½ cup (120 grams) whole milk, room temperature
¼ cup (50 grams) granulated sugar
2 tablespoons (28 grams) unsalted butter, melted
Chocolate Sauce (recipe follows)

1. Preheat oven to 350°F (180°C).
2. In the bowl of a stand mixer fitted with the paddle attachment, beat softened butter and 2 cups (440 grams) brown sugar at medium speed until fluffy, 3 to 4 minutes, stopping to scrape sides of bowl. Add eggs, one at a time, beating well after each addition. Beat in vanilla.
3. In a medium bowl, whisk together flour, 1 teaspoon (2 grams) cinnamon, baking powder, salt, and nutmeg. In a small bowl, whisk together sour cream and milk. With mixer on low speed, gradually add flour mixture to butter mixture alternately with sour cream mixture, beginning and ending with flour mixture, beating just until combined after each addition.
4. Spray a 15-cup Bundt pan with baking spray with flour. Spoon batter into prepared pan. Run a butter knife through batter 1 to 2 times, avoiding sides of pan. Gently tap pan on a kitchen towel-lined counter several times to settle batter and release any air bubbles.

5. Bake until a wooden pick inserted near center comes out clean, about 1 hour and 20 minutes, loosely covering with foil after 45 minutes of baking to prevent excess browning. Let cool in pan on a wire rack for 15 minutes. Invert cake onto wire rack, and let cool completely.
6. In a small bowl, stir together granulated sugar, remaining 2 tablespoons (28 grams) brown sugar, and remaining 1 teaspoon (2 grams) cinnamon. Working in sections, brush cake with melted butter and coat with sugar mixture, gently pressing to adhere. Serve immediately with Chocolate Sauce.

CHOCOLATE SAUCE

Makes 1½ cups

¼ cup (50 grams) granulated sugar
1½ teaspoons (4.5 grams) cornstarch
½ teaspoon instant espresso powder (optional)
¾ cup (180 grams) whole milk
¼ cup (60 grams) heavy whipping cream
2 ounces (58 grams) chopped 60% to 70% cacao bittersweet chocolate
¼ teaspoon (1 gram) vanilla extract

1. In a medium saucepan, whisk together sugar, cornstarch, and espresso (if using). Whisk in milk and cream until well combined. Bring to a boil over medium-high heat, whisking constantly; cook, whisking constantly, until mixture is thickened, 1 to 2 minutes. Remove from heat; whisk in chocolate and vanilla until melted and smooth. Let cool to room temperature.

BLACK COCOA COOKIES AND CREAM CAKE

Makes 1 (6-cup) cake

Cream-filled chocolate sandwich cookie fans, this is for you! Rich black cocoa mixes with espresso powder for a delightful chocolate kick, and a creamy cookie-filled frosting sweetly finishes it.

⅔ cup (150 grams) unsalted butter, softened
1¼ cups (250 grams) granulated sugar
2 large eggs (100 grams), room temperature
1 teaspoon (4 grams) vanilla extract
1¼ cups (156 grams) all-purpose flour
⅓ cup (25 grams) black cocoa powder
1 teaspoon (2 grams) instant espresso powder
¾ teaspoon (4 grams) baking powder
½ teaspoon (1.5 grams) kosher salt
¼ teaspoon (1.25 grams) baking soda
⅓ cup (80 grams) whole buttermilk, room temperature
Cookies and Cream Whipped Frosting (recipe follows)
Garnish: crushed cream-filled chocolate sandwich cookies

1. Preheat oven to 350°F (180°C).
2. In the bowl of a stand mixer fitted with the paddle attachment, beat butter and sugar at medium speed until light and fluffy, 3 to 4 minutes, stopping to scrape sides of bowl. Add eggs, one at a time, beating well after each addition. Beat in vanilla.
3. In a medium bowl, whisk together flour, cocoa, espresso powder, baking powder, salt, and baking soda. With mixer on low speed, gradually add flour mixture to butter mixture alternately with buttermilk, beginning and ending with flour mixture, beating until just combined after each addition.
4. Spray a Nordic Ware 6-Cup Charlotte Cake Pan with baking spray with flour. Pour batter into prepared pan.
5. Bake until a wooden pick inserted in center comes out clean, 35 to 40 minutes. Let cool in pan for 10 minutes. Remove from pan, and let cool completely on a wire rack.
6. When ready to serve, top cooled cake with Cookies and Cream Whipped Frosting. Garnish with cookies, if desired. Refrigerate in an airtight container for up to 3 days.

COOKIES AND CREAM WHIPPED FROSTING

Makes about 1¼ cups

2 ounces (57 grams) cream cheese, room temperature
¼ cup (30 grams) confectioners' sugar
½ teaspoon (2 grams) vanilla extract
¼ teaspoon kosher salt
½ cup (120 grams) cold heavy whipping cream
¼ cup (29 grams) crushed cream-filled chocolate sandwich cookies

1. In the bowl of a stand mixer fitted with the whisk attachment, beat cream cheese, confectioners' sugar, vanilla, and salt at medium-high speed until smooth, stopping to scrape sides of bowl and whisk. With mixer on medium speed, gradually add cold cream, beating until combined. Increase mixer speed to medium-high, and beat until light and fluffy, 2 to 3 minutes. Fold in cookies. Use immediately.

CARAMEL-COCONUT BUNDLETTES

Makes 6 Bundtlettes

For this twist on a classic, we kept the traditional ring shape and decadent coconut-caramel topping true to the original but replaced the standard Girl Scout Cookie with a rich, tender-crumbed vanilla cake. The result is a deliciously moist cake, covered in a rich dulce de leche-based coconut-caramel topping, all drizzled with luscious ribbons of melted dark chocolate.

½ cup (113 grams) unsalted butter, softened
¾ cup (165 grams) firmly packed dark brown sugar
¼ cup (50 grams) granulated sugar
2 large eggs (100 grams), room temperature
1 teaspoon (4 grams) vanilla extract
1⅓ cups (167 grams) all-purpose flour
½ teaspoon (1.5 grams) kosher salt
⅛ teaspoon baking soda
⅓ cup (80 grams) whole buttermilk, room temperature
1 (13.4-ounce) can (380 grams) dulce de leche
¼ cup (60 grams) whole milk, room temperature
¼ teaspoon (1 gram) coconut extract
2 cups (168 grams) sweetened flaked coconut, lightly toasted
2 ounces (56 grams) 60% cacao dark chocolate, melted

1. Preheat oven to 325°F (170°C).

2. In the bowl of a stand mixer fitted with the paddle attachment, beat butter and sugars at medium speed until fluffy, 3 to 4 minutes, stopping to scrape sides of bowl. Add eggs, one at a time, beating well after each addition. Beat in vanilla.

3. In a medium bowl, whisk together flour, salt, and baking soda. With mixer on low speed, gradually add flour mixture to butter mixture alternately with buttermilk, beginning and ending with flour mixture, beating just until combined after each addition.

4. Spray a 5-cup Bundtlette pan with baking spray with flour. Divide batter among wells (about 107 grams each). Tap pan on a kitchen towel-lined counter several times to settle batter and release any air bubbles.

5. Bake until a wooden pick inserted near center comes out clean, 15 to 20 minutes. Let cool in pan for 15 minutes. Invert Bundtlettes onto a wire rack, and let cool completely.

6. In the top of a double boiler, combine dulce de leche, milk, and coconut extract. Cook over simmering water, stirring occasionally, until fluid. Pour warm dulce de leche mixture over cooled cakes to fully coat. Press toasted coconut into tops and sides of cakes. Drizzle with melted chocolate. Refrigerate in an airtight container for up to 3 days.

HOT CHOCOLATE BUNDT CAKE

Makes 1 (10-cup) Bundt cake

Each slice reveals an intricate two-toned swirl, courtesy of alternately scooped batters that feature unsweetened and Dutch process cocoa powders. A silky Chocolate Glaze enrobes the baked cake, offering a touch of glossy shine and a boost in creamy chocolate flavor.

1	cup (227 grams) unsalted butter, softened
2	cups (400 grams) granulated sugar
4	large eggs (200 grams), room temperature
1	teaspoon (4 grams) vanilla extract
2¾	cups (344 grams) all-purpose flour
1¼	teaspoons (5.25 grams) kosher salt
1	teaspoon (2 grams) ground ancho chile pepper
½	teaspoon (2.5 grams) baking soda
1½	cups (360 grams) whole milk, room temperature
⅓	cup (25 grams) Dutch process cocoa powder, sifted
2	teaspoons (4 grams) ground cinnamon
⅓	cup (25 grams) unsweetened cocoa powder, sifted

Bittersweet Chocolate Glaze (recipe follows)

1. Preheat oven to 325°F (170°C).

2. In the bowl of a stand mixer fitted with the paddle attachment, beat butter and sugar at medium speed until fluffy, 3 to 4 minutes, stopping to scrape sides of bowl. Add eggs, one at a time, beating well after each addition. Beat in vanilla.

3. In a medium bowl, whisk together flour, salt, ancho chile pepper, and baking soda. With mixer on low speed, gradually add flour mixture to butter mixture alternately with milk, beginning and ending with flour mixture, beating just until combined after each addition. (Mixture may look curdled at certain points, but batter will come together.) Transfer half of batter (about 750 grams) to a medium bowl; gradually fold in Dutch process cocoa and cinnamon until smooth. Gradually fold unsweetened cocoa into remaining batter until smooth.

4. Spray a 10-cup Bundt pan with baking spray with flour. Using 2 (2½-tablespoon) spring-loaded scoops, alternately scoop batters into prepared pan. Tap pan on a kitchen towel-lined counter a few times to settle batter and release any air bubbles.

5. Place a heatproof wire rack on center oven rack; place pan evenly on prepared rack.

6. Bake for 50 minutes. Carefully rotate pan; bake until a wooden pick inserted near center comes out clean and an instant-read thermometer inserted near center registers 205°F (96°C), 15 to 20 minutes more. Let cool in pan for 15 minutes. Invert pan onto a wire rack. Gently tap wire rack on counter a few times to help loosen cake; remove pan, and let cake cool completely.

7. Using a serrated knife, level cooled cake, if desired. Place, cut side down, on a serving plate. Drizzle Bittersweet Chocolate Glaze onto cake.

BITTERSWEET CHOCOLATE GLAZE

Makes about 1 cup

⅔	cup (160 grams) heavy whipping cream
⅔	cup (113 grams) finely chopped 60% cacao bittersweet chocolate (about 4 ounces)

1. In a small saucepan, heat cream over medium heat just until bubbles begin to form around sides of pan. (Do not boil.) Remove from heat; add chocolate. Let stand for 5 minutes. Stir until chocolate is melted and mixture is smooth. Let cool slightly before serving.

bake it a **BUNDT**LETTE

HOT CHOCOLATE BUNDTLETTES

Makes 6 Bundtlettes

½   cup (114 grams) unsalted butter, softened
1   cup (200 grams) granulated sugar
2   large eggs (100 grams), room temperature
½   teaspoon (2 grams) vanilla extract
1¼   cups plus 2 tablespoons (172 grams) all-purpose flour
¾   teaspoon (2.6 grams) kosher salt
½   teaspoon (1 gram) ground ancho chile pepper
¼   teaspoon (1.25 grams) baking soda
¾   cup (1800 grams) whole milk, room temperature
2½   tablespoons (12.5 grams) Dutch process cocoa powder, sifted
1   teaspoon (2 grams) ground cinnamon
2½   tablespoons (12.5 grams) unsweetened cocoa powder, sifted
Bittersweet Chocolate Glaze (recipe follows)

1. Preheat oven to 325°F (170°C).
2. In the bowl of a stand mixer fitted with the paddle attachment, beat butter and sugar at medium speed until fluffy, 3 to 4 minutes, stopping to scrape sides of bowl. Add eggs, one at a time, beating well after each addition. Beat in vanilla.
3. In a medium bowl, whisk together flour, salt, ancho chile pepper, and baking soda. With mixer on low speed, gradually add flour mixture to butter mixture alternately with milk, beginning and ending with flour mixture, beating just until combined after each addition. (Mixture may look curdled at certain points, but batter will come together.) Transfer half of batter (about 375 grams) to a medium bowl; gradually fold in Dutch process cocoa and cinnamon until smooth. Gradually fold unsweetened cocoa into remaining batter until smooth.

4. Spray a 4- to 5-cup Bundtlette pan with baking spray with flour. Using 2 (1½-teaspoon) spring-loaded scoops, alternately scoop batters into prepared pan. Tap pan on a kitchen towel-lined counter a few times to settle batter and release any air bubbles.
5. Bake until a wooden pick inserted near center comes out clean and an instant-read thermometer inserted in center registers 205°F (96°C), 15 to 25 minutes. Let cool in pan for 15 minutes. Invert pan onto a wire rack. Gently tap wire rack on counter a few times to help loosen cake; remove pan, and let cake cool completely.
6. Using a serrated knife, level cooled cakes, if desired. Place, cut side down, on a serving plate. Drizzle Bittersweet Chocolate Glaze onto cooled cakes.

> **PRO TIP**
> This recipe works best with 4- to 5-cup capacity Bundtlette pans. For pans with a smaller capacity, fill wells only two-thirds full.

Bittersweet Chocolate Glaze
Makes about ½ cup

⅓   cup (80 grams) heavy whipping cream
⅓   cup (57 grams) finely chopped 60% cacao bittersweet chocolate (about 2 ounces), chopped

1. In a small saucepan, heat cream over medium heat just until bubbles begin to form around sides of pan. (Do not boil.) Remove from heat; add chocolate. Let stand for 5 minutes. Stir until chocolate is melted and mixture is smooth. Let cool slightly before serving.

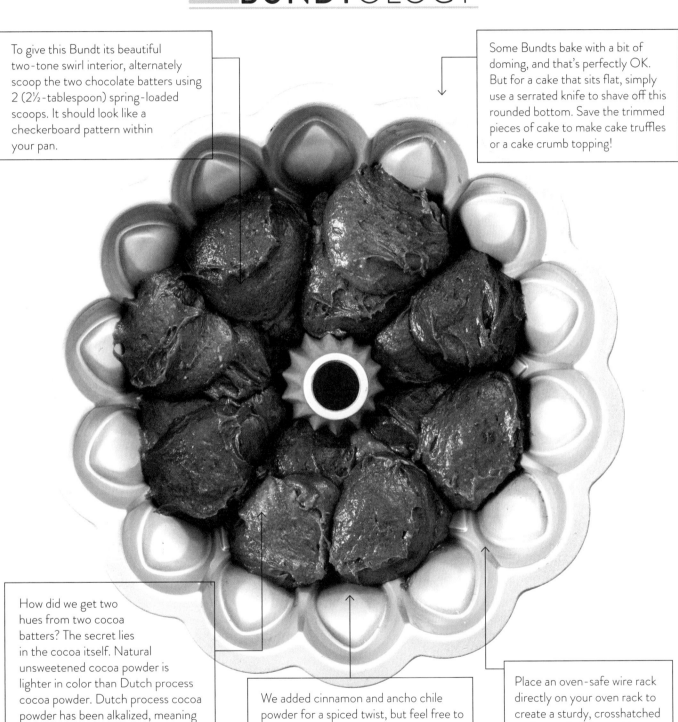

To give this Bundt its beautiful two-tone swirl interior, alternately scoop the two chocolate batters using 2 (2½-tablespoon) spring-loaded scoops. It should look like a checkerboard pattern within your pan.

Some Bundts bake with a bit of doming, and that's perfectly OK. But for a cake that sits flat, simply use a serrated knife to shave off this rounded bottom. Save the trimmed pieces of cake to make cake truffles or a cake crumb topping!

How did we get two hues from two cocoa batters? The secret lies in the cocoa itself. Natural unsweetened cocoa powder is lighter in color than Dutch process cocoa powder. Dutch process cocoa powder has been alkalized, meaning it is made less acidic, causing the natural pigments in the cocoa to darken significantly.

We added cinnamon and ancho chile powder for a spiced twist, but feel free to swap in other chocolate-friendly flavors like chai spice, peppermint extract, orange zest, almond extract, and more.

Place an oven-safe wire rack directly on your oven rack to create a sturdy, crosshatched surface to help keep this intricate Crown Bundt Pan level and stable while baking.

CHERRY CHOCOLATE AMARETTO BUNDT

Makes 1 (10-cup) Bundt cake

This fruity and chocolaty Bundt is a showstopper. Bursting with rich cherry and almond flavor, this cake is striking enough for a special occasion but simple enough for a weeknight treat, making it the baker's ultimate Bundt!

1   cup (227 grams) unsalted butter, softened
1⅓ cups (293 grams) firmly packed light brown sugar*
4   large eggs (200 grams), room temperature
1½ teaspoons (6 grams) vanilla extract
1   teaspoon (4 grams) almond extract
3   cups (375 grams) unbleached cake flour
1½ teaspoons (4.5 grams) kosher salt
1   teaspoon (5 grams) baking powder
⅔   cup (160 grams) whole buttermilk, room temperature
¼   cup (60 grams) almond liqueur
Amaretto Drunken Cherries (recipe follows)
2   ounces (57 grams) 60% cacao semisweet chocolate, chopped
Cherry Amaretto Glaze (recipe follows)
Garnish: fresh cherries

1. Preheat oven to 325°F (170°C).
2. In the bowl of a stand mixer fitted with the paddle attachment, beat butter and brown sugar at medium speed until fluffy, 3 to 4 minutes, stopping to scrape sides of bowl. Add eggs, one at a time, beating well after each addition. Beat in extracts.
3. In a medium bowl, whisk together flour, salt, and baking powder. With mixer on low speed, gradually add flour mixture to butter mixture alternately with buttermilk and liqueur, beginning and ending with flour mixture, beating just until combined after each addition. Fold in Amaretto Drunken Cherries and chocolate.
4. Spray a 10-cup Bundt pan with baking spray with flour. Spoon batter into prepared pan. Forcefully tap pan on kitchen towel-lined counter several times to settle batter and release any air bubbles.
5. Bake until a wooden pick inserted near center comes out clean or an instant-read thermometer inserted near center registers 200°F (93°C), 1 hour to 1 hour and 10 minutes. Let cool in pan for 15 minutes. Invert cake onto a wire rack, and let cool completely.
6. Place cake on serving plate. Drizzle Cherry Amaretto Glaze onto cake. Garnish with cherries, if desired.

*We used C&H® Light Brown Sugar.

AMARETTO DRUNKEN CHERRIES
Makes 1¾ cups

½   cup (100 grams) granulated sugar*
½   cup (120 grams) almond liqueur
1½ cups (242 grams) halved pitted fresh sweet cherries

1. In a small saucepan, heat sugar and liqueur over medium heat, stirring frequently, until sugar dissolves, 4 to 5 minutes. Add cherries, and cook until cherries are softened and fork-tender, 9 to 10 minutes, adjusting heat if necessary. Pour into a medium bowl; cover and refrigerate until cool, at least 1 hour or up to 4 hours. Strain through a fine-mesh sieve, reserving syrup for Cherry Amaretto Glaze.

*We used C&H® Granulated Sugar.

CHERRY AMARETTO GLAZE
Makes about ⅔ cup

1½ cups (180 grams) confectioners' sugar*
4 to 6 tablespoons (90 grams) syrup reserved from Amaretto Drunken Cherries (recipe precedes) (see Note)

1. In a small bowl, whisk together confectioners' sugar and 4 tablespoons (60 grams) reserved syrup. Add remaining 2 tablespoons (30 grams) syrup, 1 tablespoon (15 grams) at a time, until smooth. (Mixture needs to be very thick to hang on the side of the cake. Add slowly to make sure you have the right consistency.) Use immediately.

*We used C&H® Powdered Sugar.

Note: *The glaze's thickness and color will depend on how long the Amaretto Drunken Cherries were cooked.*

TUNNEL OF FUDGE CAKE

Makes 1 (15-cup) Bundt cake

An homage to the Bundt cake that started it all, this Tunnel of Fudge Cake is a true classic, composed of a rich chocolate cake with a gooey, fudgy center, all complemented by the toasted, nutty crunch of chopped pecans. For a delicious twist on the classic chocolate glaze, we drizzled the whole cake with a rich Dulce de Leche Glaze for a sweet, caramelly flair.

¾   cup (168 grams) refined coconut oil, room temperature
1   cup (227 grams) unsalted butter, softened
¾   cup (150 grams) granulated sugar
¾   cup (165 grams) firmly packed light brown sugar
6   large eggs (300 grams), room temperature
1½   teaspoons (9 grams) vanilla bean paste
1¾   cups (210 grams) confectioners' sugar
2¼   cups (281 grams) all-purpose flour
1   cup (85 grams) sifted Dutch process cocoa powder
2   teaspoons (3 grams) instant espresso powder
1½   teaspoons (4.5 grams) kosher salt
2   cups (226 grams) finely chopped toasted pecans*
Dulce de Leche Glaze (recipe follows)
Garnish: chopped toasted pecans

1. Preheat oven to 350°F (180°C).
2. In the bowl of a stand mixer, stir coconut oil by hand until smooth and softened. Add butter, granulated sugar, and brown sugar; using the paddle attachment, beat at medium-low speed just until combined. Increase mixer speed to medium, and beat until fluffy, about 3 minutes, stopping to scrape sides of bowl. Add eggs, one at a time, beating well after each addition. Beat in vanilla bean paste. With mixer on medium-low speed, beat in confectioners' sugar.
3. In a medium bowl, whisk together flour, cocoa, espresso powder, and salt. With mixer on low speed, gradually add flour mixture and finely chopped pecans to butter mixture, beating until almost combined. Fold by hand just until combined.
4. Spray a 15-cup Bundt pan with baking spray with flour. Spoon batter into prepared pan. Firmly tap pan on a kitchen towel-lined counter 10 times; smooth with an offset spatula.
5. Bake until top is shiny and set and an instant-read thermometer inserted near center registers at least 165°F (74°C), 40 to 45 minutes. Let cool in pan on a wire rack for 30 minutes. Using your fingertips, gently press down center and edges of cake. (This helps minimize the gap in the middle of the cake.) Let cool in pan on a wire rack for 1½ hours.
6. Invert cake onto wire rack, and let cool completely. Drizzle Dulce de Leche Glaze onto cooled cake. Garnish with pecans, if desired.

We used Schermer Pecans.

DULCE DE LECHE GLAZE
Makes about ½ cup

½   cup (148 grams) dulce de leche
1   tablespoon (15 grams) water, room temperature
¾   teaspoon (4.5 grams) vanilla bean paste
¼   teaspoon kosher salt

1. In a medium microwave-safe bowl, heat all ingredients on high in 10-second intervals, stirring between each, until smooth and pourable. Use immediately.

SPICED
JUST RIGHT

DIG INTO FRAGRANT CAKES FILLED
WITH WARM AND COZY SPICES

PUMPKIN DOUGHNUT BUNDT CAKE

Makes 1 (10-cup) Bundt cake

Pumpkin purée and crème fraîche are incorporated into the cake batter to yield an incredibly rich and moist cake while nutmeg, pumpkin pie spice, and cinnamon give this Bundt its quintessential warmly spiced, old-fashioned doughnut flavor. Ripples of espresso- and cinnamon-spiked brown sugar streusel swirl throughout to give an added kick of sweetness and spice while also paying homage to the beloved flavors of the famous pumpkin spice latte. Gorgeously ornate yet incredibly easy to make and share, this elegant amber-hued cake will quickly become a new fall favorite.

Filling:

3 tablespoons (24 grams) all-purpose flour
3 tablespoons (42 grams) firmly packed light brown sugar
1 tablespoon (4 grams) instant espresso powder
½ teaspoon (1 gram) ground cinnamon
⅛ teaspoon kosher salt
1 tablespoon (14 grams) unsalted butter, room temperature

Batter:

1 (15-ounce) can (425 grams) pumpkin (about 1¾ cups)
1⅓ cups (293 grams) firmly packed light brown sugar
¾ cup (150 grams) granulated sugar
¾ cup (180 grams) crème fraîche, room temperature
⅔ cup (149 grams) vegetable oil
¼ cup (57 grams) unsalted butter, melted
3 large eggs (150 grams), room temperature
2 teaspoons (12 grams) vanilla bean paste
2⅓ cups (292 grams) all-purpose flour
2 teaspoons (10 grams) baking powder
1½ teaspoons (4.5 grams) kosher salt
1½ teaspoons (3 grams) ground nutmeg
1 teaspoon (2 grams) pumpkin pie spice
¾ teaspoon (1.5 grams) ground cinnamon
½ teaspoon (2.5 grams) baking soda

Topping:

¼ cup (50 grams) granulated sugar
2 tablespoons (28 grams) firmly packed light brown sugar
¾ teaspoon (1.5 grams) ground cinnamon
½ teaspoon (1 gram) instant espresso powder
¼ teaspoon ground nutmeg
2 tablespoons (28 grams) unsalted butter, melted

1. Preheat oven to 325°F (170°C).

2. For filling: In a small bowl, stir together flour, brown sugar, espresso powder, cinnamon, and salt. Add butter, and rub in by hand until mixture is sandy and well combined.

3. For batter: In a large bowl, whisk together pumpkin, brown sugar, granulated sugar, crème fraîche, oil, melted butter, eggs, and vanilla bean paste.

4. In a medium bowl, whisk together flour, baking powder, salt, nutmeg, pie spice, cinnamon, and baking soda. Gradually whisk flour mixture into pumpkin mixture until smooth and well combined.

5. Spray a 10-cup Bundt pan with baking spray with flour. Spoon one-third of batter into prepared pan (about 2¼ cups or 567 grams). Tap pan on a kitchen towel-lined counter several times to settle batter and release any air bubbles. Using a small spoon, sprinkle half of filling (3½ to 4 tablespoons or about 43 grams) in a ring on top of batter in pan, layering and spreading mixture as needed and leaving about a ¼-inch border around edges. Top with one-third of batter. Tap pan on a kitchen towel-lined counter a few times to settle batter and release any air bubbles. Top with a ring of remaining filling; cover with remaining batter. Tap on a kitchen towel-lined counter several times to settle batter and release any air bubbles.

6. Bake for 55 minutes. Rotate pan, loosely cover with foil, and bake until a wooden pick inserted near center comes out clean and an instant-read thermometer inserted near center registers 200°F (93°C) to 205°F (96°C), 20 to 25 minutes more. Let cool in pan for 15 minutes. Invert cake onto a wire rack, and let cool completely.

7. For topping: In a small bowl, stir together granulated sugar, brown sugar, cinnamon, espresso powder, and nutmeg. Brush cake with melted butter; sprinkle with sugar mixture, gently pressing to adhere, if needed. Serve immediately.

bake it a **BUNDT**LETTE

PUMPKIN DOUGHNUT BUNDTLETTES

Makes 6 Bundtlettes

Filling:

4	teaspoons (12 grams) all-purpose flour
4	teaspoons (20 grams) firmly packed light brown sugar
1½	teaspoons (2 grams) instant espresso powder
¼	teaspoon ground cinnamon

Pinch kosher salt

1½	teaspoons (7.5 grams) unsalted butter, room temperature

Batter:

¾	cup plus 2 tablespoons (196 grams) canned pumpkin
½	cup plus 1 tablespoon (124 grams) firmly packed light brown sugar
⅓	cup (67 grams) granulated sugar
⅓	cup (80 grams) crème fraîche, room temperature
⅓	cup (75 grams) vegetable oil
1	large egg (50 grams), room temperature
1	large egg yolk (19 grams), room temperature
2	tablespoons (28 grams) unsalted butter, melted
1	teaspoon (6 grams) vanilla bean paste
1	cup (125 grams) all-purpose flour
1	teaspoon (5 grams) baking powder
¾	teaspoon (2.25 grams) kosher salt
¾	teaspoon (1.5 grams) ground nutmeg
½	teaspoon (1 gram) pumpkin pie spice
¼	teaspoon (1.25 grams) baking soda
¼	teaspoon ground cinnamon

Topping:

2	tablespoons (24 grams) granulated sugar
1	tablespoon (14 grams) firmly packed light brown sugar
¼	teaspoon ground cinnamon
¼	teaspoon instant espresso powder
⅛	teaspoon ground nutmeg
2	tablespoons (28 grams) unsalted butter, melted

1. Preheat oven to 325°F (170°C).

2. For filling: In a small bowl, stir together flour, brown sugar, espresso powder, cinnamon, and salt. Add butter, and rub in by hand until mixture is sandy and well combined.

3. For batter: In a large bowl, whisk together pumpkin, brown sugar, granulated sugar, crème fraîche, oil, egg, egg yolk, melted butter, and vanilla bean paste.

4. In a medium bowl, whisk together flour, baking powder, salt, nutmeg, pie spice, baking soda, and cinnamon. Gradually whisk flour mixture into pumpkin mixture just until smooth and well combined.

5. Spray a 4- to 5-cup Bundtlette pan with baking spray with flour. Divide one-third of batter among prepared wells (about 2½ tablespoons or 42 grams each). Tap pan on a kitchen towel-lined counter a few times to settle batter and release any air bubbles. Divide half of filling (about 2 tablespoons or about 20 grams) among wells, leaving about a ¼-inch border around edges. (It's OK if some filling touches edges of pan.) Top with one-third of batter; spread batter to cover filling, and tap pan on a kitchen towel-lined counter just a few times to settle batter and release any air bubbles. Sprinkle with remaining filling; cover with remaining batter, spreading to cover filling. Tap on a kitchen towel-lined counter just a few times to settle batter and release any air bubbles.

6. Bake until a wooden pick inserted near center comes out clean, 12 to 20 minutes. Let cool in pan for 15 minutes. Invert Bundtlettes onto a wire rack, and let cool completely.

7. For topping: In a shallow dish, whisk together granulated sugar, brown sugar, cinnamon, espresso powder, and nutmeg. Brush Bundtlettes with melted butter; dredge in sugar mixture to coat. Serve immediately.

bake FROM SCRATCH™
BUNDTOLOGY

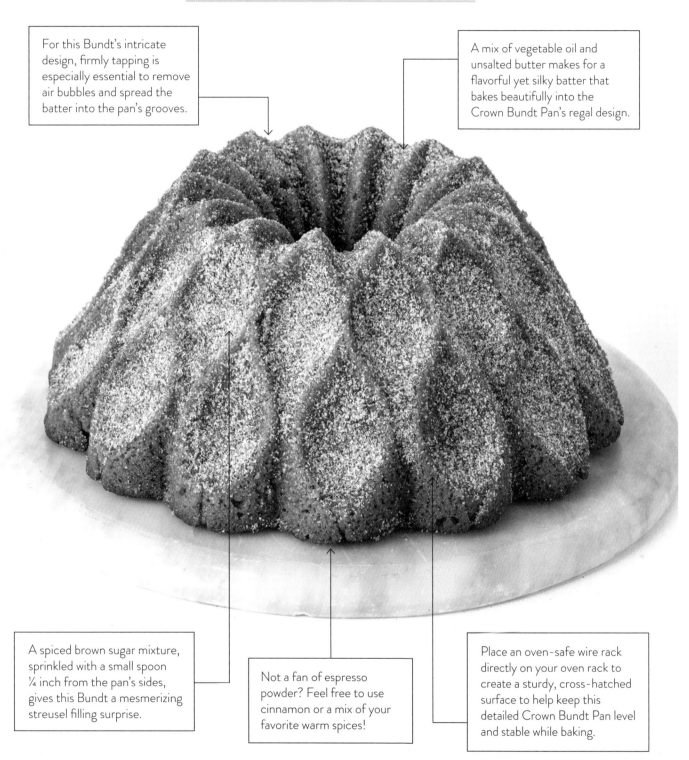

For this Bundt's intricate design, firmly tapping is especially essential to remove air bubbles and spread the batter into the pan's grooves.

A mix of vegetable oil and unsalted butter makes for a flavorful yet silky batter that bakes beautifully into the Crown Bundt Pan's regal design.

A spiced brown sugar mixture, sprinkled with a small spoon ¼ inch from the pan's sides, gives this Bundt a mesmerizing streusel filling surprise.

Not a fan of espresso powder? Feel free to use cinnamon or a mix of your favorite warm spices!

Place an oven-safe wire rack directly on your oven rack to create a sturdy, cross-hatched surface to help keep this detailed Crown Bundt Pan level and stable while baking.

CARROT BUNDT CAKE

Makes 1 (10-cup) Bundt cake

You've never had a carrot cake like this! Perfectly blended spices join with sweet carrots, earthy pecans, and chewy raisins. A gorgeous cream cheese topping adorns this delightful masterpiece, creating a dessert worthy of any dinner table.

2   cups (250 grams) all-purpose flour
1   cup (200 grams) granulated sugar
⅔   cup (147 grams) firmly packed light brown sugar
4   teaspoons (8 grams) ground cinnamon
2   teaspoons (10 grams) baking powder
1½   teaspoons (3 grams) ground ginger
1   teaspoon (3 grams) kosher salt
1   teaspoon (2 grams) ground nutmeg
½   teaspoon (2.5 grams) baking soda
1   cup (224 grams) neutral oil
½   cup (120 grams) whole buttermilk, room temperature
4   large eggs (200 grams), room temperature
1   tablespoon (13 grams) vanilla extract
3   cups (300 grams) lightly packed shredded carrots
1   cup (120 grams) finely chopped toasted pecans
½   cup (80 grams) golden raisins
Cream Cheese Frosting (recipe follows)
Garnish: finely chopped toasted pecans

1. Preheat oven to 350°F (180°C).
2. In a large bowl, whisk together flour, sugars, cinnamon, baking powder, ginger, salt, nutmeg, and baking soda.
3. In a medium bowl, whisk together oil, buttermilk, eggs, and vanilla. Add oil mixture to flour mixture, whisking just until combined. Fold in carrots, pecans, and raisins.
4. Spray a 10-cup Bundt pan with baking spray with flour. Lightly sprinkle flour into pan to coat; tap pan on counter to remove excess flour. Pour batter into prepared pan. Tap pan on a kitchen towel-lined counter several times to settle batter and release any air bubbles.
5. Bake until a wooden pick inserted near center comes out clean and an instant-read thermometer registers 200°F (93°C) and 205°F (96°C), 1 hour and 5 minutes to 1 hour and 10 minutes. Let cool in pan for 15 minutes. Invert cake onto a wire rack, and let cool completely.
6. Spread Cream Cheese Frosting onto cooled cake. Garnish with pecans, if desired. Cover and refrigerate for up to 3 days.

CREAM CHEESE FROSTING

Makes about ½ cup

4   ounces (113 grams) cream cheese, softened
¼   cup (30 grams) confectioners' sugar
2 to 3 tablespoons (30 to 45 grams) whole milk

1. In the bowl of a stand mixer fitted with the paddle attachment, beat cream cheese at medium-low speed until smooth and creamy, about 1 minute. Add confectioners' sugar, beating until combined. Add milk, 1 tablespoon (15 grams) at a time, beating until thick but when a spoon is dragged through center, icing slowly falls back into space left behind, stopping to scrape sides of bowl. Use immediately.

BAKLAVA BUNDT CAKE

Makes 1 (10-cup) Bundt cake

Honeyed and sweet, with a satisfying crunch, this warm and rich Baklava Bundt Cake is the ultimate cozy and comforting bake to kick off the fall baking season. Almonds and pistachios are coated in honey and butter to create the candied nuts on top of the cake, and the cake batter is enriched with Greek yogurt for a moist, tender crumb that's studded with more crunchy nuts.

¾ cup (105 grams) roughly chopped almonds
¾ cup (105 grams) roughly chopped pistachios
½ cup (170 grams) honey, divided
⅓ cup (76 grams) unsalted butter, melted
1 teaspoon (2.25 grams) kosher salt, divided
¾ cup (170 grams) unsalted butter, softened
¾ cup (150 grams) granulated sugar
½ cup (110 grams) firmly packed light brown sugar
3 large eggs (200 grams), room temperature
2 teaspoons (8 grams) vanilla extract
2¼ cups (281 grams) all-purpose flour
1 teaspoon (5 grams) baking powder
½ teaspoon (2.5 grams) baking soda
½ cup (120 grams) full-fat Greek yogurt, room temperature
¼ cup (60 grams) whole milk, room temperature
Nut Filling (recipe follows)

1. Preheat oven to 325°F (170°C). Spray a 10-cup Bundt pan with baking spray with flour.

2. In a medium bowl, stir together almonds, pistachios, ¼ cup (85 grams) honey, melted butter, and ¼ teaspoon salt until well combined. Spoon into bottom of prepared pan, pressing with a spatula until even and packed. (Butter will resolidify while you prepare batter.)

3. In the bowl of a stand mixer fitted with the paddle attachment, beat softened butter, sugars, and remaining ¼ cup (85 grams) honey at medium speed until fluffy, 3 to 4 minutes, stopping to scrape sides of bowl. Add eggs, one at a time, beating well after each addition. Beat in vanilla.

4. In a medium bowl, whisk together flour, baking powder, baking soda, and remaining ¾ teaspoon (2.25 grams) salt. In a small bowl, whisk together yogurt and milk. With mixer on low speed, gradually add flour mixture to butter mixture alternately with yogurt mixture, beginning and ending with flour mixture, beating just until combined after each addition. (Batter will be thick.) Spoon 3 cups (700 grams) batter into prepared pan on top of nut mixture. Tap pan on a kitchen towel-lined counter several times to spread batter into grooves and release any air bubbles. Sprinkle Nut Filling on top of batter in pan, leaving a ¼-inch border on all sides. Spoon remaining batter (about 416 grams) on top of filling in small dollops. Using a small offset spatula, smooth top. Tap pan on a kitchen towel-lined counter several times to spread batter into grooves and release any air bubbles.

5. Bake until a wooden pick inserted near center comes out clean or an instant-read thermometer inserted near center registers 200°F (93°C) to 205°F (96°C), 55 minutes to 1 hour and 5 minutes, covering with foil after 30 minutes of baking to prevent excess browning. Let cool in pan for 15 minutes. (Do not let cool in pan for longer or the nuts will stick to the pan.) Using a small offset spatula, loosen cake from center of pan. Invert cake pan onto a wire rack. Let cool for at least 45 minutes, and serve warm, or let cool completely, and serve at room temperature.

NUT FILLING
Makes about ½ cup

2½ tablespoons (22 grams) finely chopped almonds
2½ tablespoons (22 grams) finely chopped pistachios
2 tablespoons (28 grams) firmly packed light brown sugar

1. In a small bowl, stir together all ingredients until combined.

OATMEAL CREAM BUNDT CAKE

Makes 1 (10-cup) Bundt cake

We took the nostalgic oatmeal cream pie and transformed it into a golden-brown Oatmeal Cream Bundt Cake, twirled and swirled with a soft, tangy cream cheese mixture. Spiced with cinnamon and accented with cocoa powder, this cake will take you on sweet journey back in time.

8   ounces (226 grams) cream cheese, softened
3   cups (375 grams) plus 2 tablespoons (16 grams) all-purpose flour, divided
¾   cup (150 grams) plus 2 tablespoons (24 grams) granulated sugar, divided
5   large eggs (250 grams), room temperature and divided
1   cup (100 grams) old-fashioned oats
½   cup (80 grams) roughly chopped raisins
3   tablespoons (15 grams) unsweetened cocoa powder
2   teaspoons (4 grams) ground cinnamon
1½   teaspoons (4.5 grams) kosher salt
½   teaspoon (2.5 grams) baking soda
1   cup (227 grams) unsalted butter, softened
1   cup (220 grams) firmly packed light brown sugar
1   teaspoon (4 grams) vanilla extract
1¼   cups (300 grams) whole buttermilk, room temperature
Vanilla Glaze (recipe follows)

1. In the bowl of a stand mixer fitted with the paddle attachment, beat cream cheese, 2 tablespoons (16 grams) flour, and 2 tablespoons (24 grams) granulated sugar at medium speed until well combined, 1 to 2 minutes, stopping to scrape sides of bowl. Add 1 egg (50 grams); beat until well combined. Transfer mixture to a small bowl, and refrigerate for 20 minutes.

2. Preheat oven to 350°F (180°C).

3. In the work bowl of a food processor, pulse oats until small and uniform in size but not too powdery. Add raisins, and pulse until finely chopped. Transfer to a medium bowl, and whisk in cocoa, cinnamon, salt, baking soda, and remaining 3 cups (375 grams) flour.

4. Clean bowl of stand mixer and paddle attachment. Using the paddle attachment, beat butter, brown sugar, and remaining ¾ cup (150 grams) granulated sugar at medium-low speed just until combined; increase mixer speed to medium, and beat until fluffy, 3 to 4 minutes, stopping to scrape sides of bowl. Add remaining 4 eggs (200 grams), one at a time, beating until well combined after each addition. (Mixture may look slightly broken at this point, but batter will come together.) Beat in vanilla. With mixer on low speed, gradually add oats mixture to butter mixture alternately with buttermilk, beginning and ending with oats mixture, beating just until combined after each addition and stopping to scrape sides of bowl.

5. Spray a 10-cup Bundt pan with baking spray with flour. Spoon 2¼ cups (520 grams) batter into prepared pan. Tap pan on a kitchen towel-lined counter several times to settle batter and release any air bubbles. Using the back of a spoon, make a ½-inch-deep, 1-inch-wide trench in center of batter in pan, leaving a ¼- to ½-inch border around edges. Spoon 3 cups (693 grams) remaining batter into a large pastry bag; cut a ½-inch opening in tip. Pipe a border of batter around outer and inner edges of pan. Spoon small dollops of cream cheese mixture and pipe alternating small dollops of batter into trench in batter in pan. After completing 1 ring in pan, pipe border higher, if needed, and pipe batter over cream cheese dollops and vice versa until cream cheese mixture is all used up. Drag a wooden pick through center of each dollop to swirl into batter and gently tap pan on a kitchen towel-lined counter to release any air bubbles. Pipe and gently spread remaining batter on top, covering cream cheese mixture. (Pan will be full. Do not tap pan.)

6. Bake until a wooden pick inserted near center comes out clean and an instant-read thermometer inserted near center registers 205°F (93°C), 1 hour and 10 minutes to 1 hour and 15 minutes. (Top will have a slight jiggle to it because of the filling.) Let cool in pan for 20 minutes. Using a small offset spatula, gently loosen cake from center of pan. Invert cake onto a wire rack placed over a rimmed baking sheet. Let cool completely. Transfer to a serving plate, and slowly spoon Vanilla Glaze on top before serving.

VANILLA GLAZE

Makes ⅓ cup

1   cup (120 grams) confectioners' sugar
4   teaspoons (20 grams) water
¼   teaspoon (1 gram) vanilla extract

1. In a medium bowl, whisk together ¾ cup (90 grams) confectioners' sugar and 4 teaspoons (20 grams) water until smooth. Add vanilla and remaining ¼ cup (30 grams) confectioners' sugar, and whisk until combined. (Glaze will be thick.) Let stand for 5 minutes before using.

OCRACOKE ISLAND FIG CAKE

Makes 1 (10-cup) Bundt cake

This cake, originally from North Carolina's Outer Banks, makes use of the luscious fig trees that ripen in midsummer to produce an abundance of fruit on Ocracoke Island. Our version of this rich cake is made with homemade fig jam and studded with pecans.

3	large eggs (150 grams), room temperature
1¼	cups (250 grams) granulated sugar
1	cup (224 grams) vegetable oil
1	cup (308 grams) Quick Fig Jam (recipe follows)
¼	cup (55 grams) firmly packed light brown sugar
½	teaspoon (1 gram) packed lemon zest
2	cups (250 grams) all-purpose flour
1¼	teaspoons (3.75 grams) kosher salt
1	teaspoon (2 grams) ground nutmeg
1	teaspoon (2 grams) ground cinnamon
¾	teaspoon (1.5 grams) ground allspice
¼	teaspoon ground black pepper
1	tablespoon (15 grams) warm water (90°F/32°C)
1	teaspoon (5 grams) baking soda
½	cup (120 grams) whole buttermilk, room temperature
2½	teaspoons (15 grams) vanilla bean paste
1	cup (113 grams) chopped toasted pecans

Buttermilk Glaze (recipe follow)
Garnish: halved fresh figs, finely chopped toasted pecans

1. Preheat oven to 350°F (180°C).

2. In the bowl of a stand mixer fitted with the paddle attachment, beat eggs at medium speed until smooth and well combined, about 2 minutes. Add granulated sugar, oil, Quick Fig Jam, brown sugar, and lemon zest; beat until thickened and well combined, 2 to 3 minutes, stopping to scrape sides of bowl.

3. In a medium bowl, whisk together flour, salt, nutmeg, cinnamon, allspice, and pepper. In a small bowl, stir together 1 tablespoon (15 grams) warm water and baking soda; add buttermilk and vanilla bean paste, stirring until well combined. With mixer on low speed, gradually add flour mixture to egg mixture alternately with buttermilk mixture, beginning and ending with flour mixture, beating until nearly combined. Fold in chopped pecans.

4. Spray a 10-cup Bundt pan (see Notes) with baking spray with flour. Pour batter into prepared pan. Firmly tap pan on a kitchen towel-lined counter several times to settle batter and release any air bubbles.

5. Bake until a wooden pick inserted near center comes out clean, 55 minutes to 1 hour and 5 minutes, loosely covering with foil during final 5 minutes of baking to prevent excess browning. Let cool in pan on a wire rack for 15 minutes. Using a butter knife or a small offset spatula, gently loosen sides and center of cake from pan. Invert cake onto a wire rack, and let cool completely.

6. Spoon and spread Buttermilk Glaze onto cooled cake as desired. Garnish with figs and pecans, if desired. Refrigerate in an airtight container for up to 3 days.

Notes: *This recipe works best in a Bundt pan with a more rounded, open, less detailed design.*

To help keep Bundt pan level while baking, place a wire rack directly on oven rack to create a crosshatched surface.

QUICK FIG JAM

Makes 3 to 4 cups

2	pounds (908 grams) fresh Black Mission figs, stemmed and chopped (about 6 cups)
2	cups (400 grams) granulated sugar
6	(¼-inch-thick) slices lemon (about 60 grams), seeded
4	teaspoons (20 grams) fresh lemon juice

1. In a medium saucepan, bring all ingredients to a boil over medium-high heat. Cook, stirring frequently, for 5 minutes. Reduce heat to medium-low; cook, stirring frequently and mashing figs with a potato masher, until thickened and an instant-read thermometer registers 220°F (104°C), 25 to 35 minutes. Remove from heat, and let cool for 30 minutes. Refrigerate in an airtight container for up to 1 week.

BUTTERMILK GLAZE

Makes about ¾ cup

1¾	cups (210 grams) confectioners' sugar
3	tablespoons (45 grams) whole buttermilk
1	tablespoon (14 grams) unsalted butter, melted
½	teaspoon (3 grams) vanilla bean paste
¼	teaspoon kosher salt

1. In a medium bowl, whisk together all ingredients until smooth. Use immediately.

PUMPKIN SPICE CAKE

Makes 1 (10-cup) Bundt cake

In this eye-catching cake, creamy pumpkin is mixed with brown sugar and vanilla paste to create the perfect amount of seasonal sweetness while sour cream serves to balance and turn up the tang. Brushed with butter and sprinkled with sugar and spice, this fall classic will give you all the cozy feelings.

1   (15-ounce) can (425 grams) pumpkin (about 1¾ cups)
1   cups (293 grams) firmly packed light brown sugar
¾   cup (150 grams) granulated sugar
¾   cup (180 grams) sour cream, room temperature
⅔   cup (149 grams) vegetable oil
¼   cup (57 grams) plus 1 tablespoon (14 grams) unsalted butter, melted and divided
3   large eggs (150 grams), room temperature
2   teaspoons (12 grams) vanilla bean paste
2⅓ cups (292 grams) all-purpose flour
2   teaspoons (10 grams) baking powder
1½ teaspoons (4.5 grams) kosher salt
1½ teaspoons (3 grams) ground nutmeg
1   teaspoon (2 grams) pumpkin pie spice
¾   teaspoon (1.5 grams) ground cinnamon
½   teaspoon (2.5 grams) baking soda
Brown Sugar Topping (recipe follows)

1. Preheat oven to 325°F (170°C).
2. In a large bowl, whisk together pumpkin, brown sugar, granulated sugar, sour cream, oil, ¼ cup (57 grams) melted butter, eggs, and vanilla bean paste.
3. In a medium bowl, whisk together flour, baking powder, salt, nutmeg, pie spice, cinnamon, and baking soda. Gradually whisk flour mixture into pumpkin mixture until smooth and well combined.
4. Spray a 10-cup Bundt pan with baking spray with flour. Spoon batter into prepared pan. Tap pan on a kitchen towel-lined counter several times to settle batter and release any air bubbles.
5. Bake until a wooden pick inserted near center comes out clean and an instant-read thermometer inserted near center registers 200°F (93°C) to 205°F (96°C), 1 hour to 1 hour and 15 minutes. Let cool in pan for 15 minutes. Invert cake onto a wire rack, and let cool completely.
6. Brush cake lightly with remaining 1 tablespoon (14 grams) melted butter; sprinkle Brown Sugar Topping onto cake, gently pressing to adhere. Serve immediately.

BROWN SUGAR TOPPING
Makes about 3 tablespoons

2   tablespoons (24 grams) granulated sugar
1   tablespoon (14 grams) firmly packed light brown sugar
½   teaspoon (1 gram) ground cinnamon
⅛   teaspoon ground nutmeg

1. In a small bowl, whisk together all ingredients until combined.

PANCAKE BUNDT CAKE

Makes 1 (10-cup) Bundt cake

Gone are the days of standing in front of a hot buttered skillet dishing out pancakes one by one. By placing the light golden batter into one gorgeous vessel, your favorite breakfast item magically transforms into a light and fluffy sliceable cake. Whether feeding loved ones or savoring the cake over a few days, this Bundt is versatile enough to be enjoyed for brunch, dessert, or a luxurious afternoon snack.

3   cups (375 grams) plus 2 tablespoons (16 grams) all-purpose flour, divided
8   tablespoons (112 grams) unsalted butter, melted and divided
½   cup (100 grams) granulated sugar
3¾   teaspoons (18.75 grams) baking powder
1¼   teaspoons (3.75 grams) kosher salt
¼   teaspoon ground nutmeg
1¼   cups (300 grams) heavy whipping cream, room temperature
1   cup (240 grams) water, room temperature
3   large eggs (150 grams), room temperature
1½   teaspoons (9 grams) vanilla bean paste
Maple Simple Syrup (recipe follows)
Brown Sugar-Maple Glaze (recipe follows)

1. Preheat oven to 350°F (180°C).
2. In a small bowl, stir together 2 tablespoons (16 grams) flour and 2 tablespoons (28 grams) melted butter until well combined. Using a pastry brush, spread flour mixture all over inside of a 10-cup Bundt pan, being sure to evenly get into grooves.
3. In a large bowl, whisk together sugar, baking powder, salt, nutmeg, and remaining 3 cups (375 grams) flour.
4. In a medium bowl, whisk together cream, 1 cup (240 grams) water, eggs, and vanilla bean paste; whisk in remaining 6 tablespoons (84 grams) melted butter. Add cream mixture to sugar mixture; whisk just until combined and no large flour pockets remain. (Mixture will still be lumpy; do not overmix.) Pour batter into prepared pan. Firmly tap pan on a kitchen towel-lined counter several times to settle batter and release any air bubbles.

5. Bake until a wooden pick inserted near center comes out clean and an instant-read thermometer inserted near center registers 200°F (93°C), 35 to 40 minutes. Let cool in pan for 10 minutes. Invert cake onto a wire rack placed over a rimmed baking sheet. Generously brush Maple Simple Syrup all over warm cake until all of mixture is used up. Let cake cool for 20 minutes.
6. Drizzle Brown Sugar-Maple Glaze onto cake as desired. Serve warm.

MAPLE SIMPLE SYRUP
Makes about ⅓ cup

¼   cup (85 grams) maple syrup
1   tablespoon (12 grams) granulated sugar
1   tablespoon (15 grams) water
¼   teaspoon (1 gram) maple extract

1. In a small microwave-safe bowl, whisk together maple syrup, granulated sugar, and 1 tablespoon (15 grams) water until well combined. Heat on high in 10- to 20-second intervals, whisking between each, until sugar dissolves. Whisk in maple extract.

BROWN SUGAR-MAPLE GLAZE
Makes about ¾ cup

½   cup (110 grams) firmly packed dark brown sugar
6   tablespoons (84 grams) unsalted butter, softened
2   tablespoons (30 grams) heavy whipping cream
1   teaspoon (7 grams) maple syrup
½   teaspoon (1.5 grams) kosher salt
1   teaspoon (4 grams) maple extract
½   teaspoon (3 grams) vanilla bean paste

1. In a small saucepan, bring brown sugar, butter, cream, maple syrup, and salt to a boil over medium-high heat, stirring frequently. Cook, stirring constantly, for 2 minutes. Remove from heat; stir in extract and vanilla paste.

Note: *If glaze starts to get too cool and thick, heat in a microwave-safe bowl on high in 10-second intervals, stirring between each, until desired consistency is reached.*

bake it a **BUNDT**LETTE

PANCAKE BUNDTLETTES

Makes 6 Bundtlettes

2   cups (250 grams) plus 1 tablespoon (8 grams) all-purpose flour, divided
¼   cup (57 grams) plus 1 tablespoon (14 grams) unsalted butter, melted and divided
⅓   cup (67 grams) granulated sugar
2½   teaspoons (12.5 grams) baking powder
¾   teaspoon (2.25 grams) kosher salt
⅛   teaspoon ground nutmeg
¾   cup plus 1 tablespoon (195 grams) heavy whipping cream, room temperature
⅔   cup (160 grams) water, room temperature
2   large eggs (100 grams), room temperature
1   teaspoon (6 grams) vanilla bean paste
Maple Simple Syrup (recipe follows)
Brown Sugar-Maple Glaze (recipe follows)

1. Preheat oven to 350°F (180°C).
2. In a small bowl, stir together 1 tablespoon (8 grams) flour and 1 tablespoon (14 grams) melted butter until well combined. Using a pastry brush, spread flour mixture all over inside of a 5-cup Bundtlette pan (see Note), being sure to evenly get into grooves.
3. In a large bowl, whisk together sugar, baking powder, salt, nutmeg, and remaining 2 cups (250 grams) flour.
4. In a medium bowl, whisk together cream, ⅔ cup (160 grams) water, eggs, and vanilla bean paste. Whisk in remaining ¼ cup (57 grams) melted butter. Add cream mixture to sugar mixture; whisk just until combined and no large flour pockets remain. (Mixture will still be lumpy; do not overmix.) Divide batter among wells. Firmly tap pan on a kitchen towel-lined counter several times to settle batter and release any air bubbles.
5. Bake until a wooden pick inserted near center comes out clean, 10 to 13 minutes. Let cool in pan for 10 minutes. Invert Bundtlettes onto a wire rack placed over a rimmed baking sheet. Generously brush Maple Simple Syrup all over warm cakes until all simple syrup is used. Let cool for 20 minutes.
6. Drizzle Brown Sugar-Maple Glaze onto Bundtlettes. Serve warm.

Note: *This recipe fits 5-cup-capacity Bundtlette pans. For Bundtlette pans with smaller capacities, fill wells only two-thirds full.*

Maple Simple Syrup
Makes about ⅓ cup

¼   cup (85 grams) maple syrup
1   tablespoon (12 grams) granulated sugar
1   tablespoon (15 grams) water
¼   teaspoon (1 gram) maple extract

1. In a small microwave-safe bowl, whisk together maple syrup, sugar, and 1 tablespoon (15 grams) water until well combined. Heat on high in 10- to 20-second intervals, whisking between each, until sugar dissolves. Whisk in maple extract.

Brown Sugar-Maple Glaze
Makes about ¾ cup

½   cup (110 grams) firmly packed dark brown sugar
6   tablespoons (84 grams) unsalted butter, softened
2   tablespoons (30 grams) heavy whipping cream
1   teaspoon (7 grams) maple syrup
½   teaspoon (1.5 grams) kosher salt
1   teaspoon (4 grams) maple extract
½   teaspoon (3 grams) vanilla bean paste

1. In a small saucepan, bring brown sugar, butter, cream, maple syrup, and salt to a boil over medium-high heat, stirring frequently. Cook, stirring constantly, for 2 minutes. Remove from heat; stir in extract and vanilla paste.

Note: *If glaze starts to get too cool and thick, heat in a microwave-safe bowl on high in 10-second intervals, stirring between each, until desired consistency is reached.*

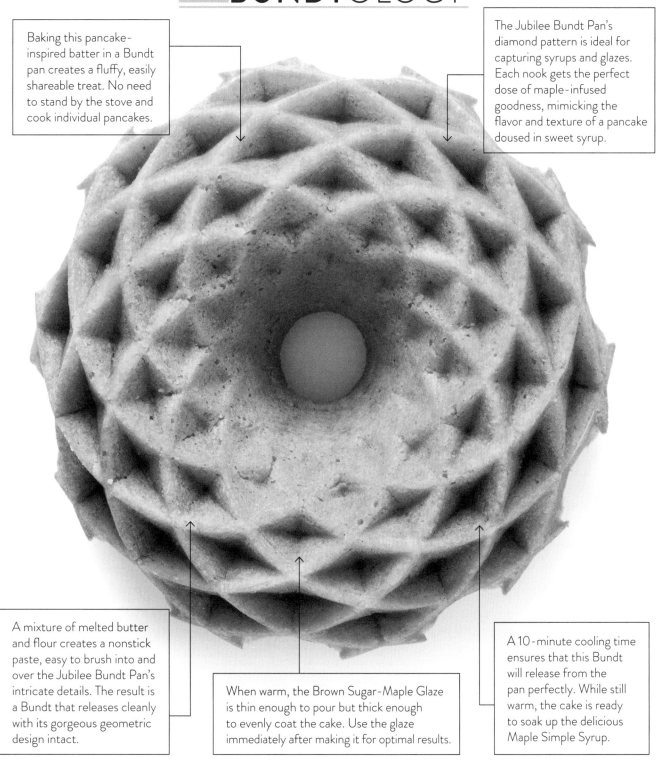

Baking this pancake-inspired batter in a Bundt pan creates a fluffy, easily shareable treat. No need to stand by the stove and cook individual pancakes.

The Jubilee Bundt Pan's diamond pattern is ideal for capturing syrups and glazes. Each nook gets the perfect dose of maple-infused goodness, mimicking the flavor and texture of a pancake doused in sweet syrup.

A mixture of melted butter and flour creates a nonstick paste, easy to brush into and over the Jubilee Bundt Pan's intricate details. The result is a Bundt that releases cleanly with its gorgeous geometric design intact.

When warm, the Brown Sugar-Maple Glaze is thin enough to pour but thick enough to evenly coat the cake. Use the glaze immediately after making it for optimal results.

A 10-minute cooling time ensures that this Bundt will release from the pan perfectly. While still warm, the cake is ready to soak up the delicious Maple Simple Syrup.

EARL GREY-ORANGE BUNDT CAKE

Makes 1 (12-cup) Bundt cake

This pretty cake takes the flavors of a classic tea and turns them into a beautifully swirled Bundt cake. Filled with bright orange zest and a smooth cream cheese filling, this cake will be the highlight of your next afternoon tea.

8 ounces (226 grams) cream cheese, softened
3 cups (375 grams) plus 2 tablespoons (16 grams) all-purpose flour, divided
1⅔ cups (334 grams) plus 2 tablespoons (24 grams) granulated sugar, divided
5 large eggs (250 grams), room temperature and divided
1 cup (227 grams) unsalted butter, softened
½ cup (110 grams) firmly packed light brown sugar
1 teaspoon (4 grams) tightly packed orange zest
2 tablespoons (16 grams) plus 1 teaspoon (4 grams) finely ground Earl Grey tea (see Note), divided
1 teaspoon (3 grams) kosher salt
½ teaspoon (2.5 grams) baking soda
1¼ cups (300 grams) whole buttermilk, room temperature
2 tablespoons (28 grams) unsalted butter, melted

1. Preheat oven to 350°F (180°C).
2. In the bowl of a stand mixer fitted with the paddle attachment, beat cream cheese, 2 tablespoons (16 grams) flour, and 2 tablespoons (24 grams) granulated sugar at medium speed until well combined, 1 to 2 minutes, stopping to scrape sides of bowl. Beat in 1 egg (50 grams) until well combined. Transfer mixture to a small bowl; refrigerate for 20 minutes.
3. Clean bowl of stand mixer and paddle attachment. Using the paddle attachment, beat softened butter, 1⅓ cups (267 grams) granulated sugar, brown sugar, and orange zest at medium-low speed just until combined; increase mixer speed to medium, and beat until fluffy, 3 to 4 minutes, stopping to scrape sides of bowl. Add remaining 4 eggs (200 grams), one at a time, beating until well combined after each addition. (Mixture may look slightly broken at this point, but batter will come together.)
4. In a large bowl, whisk together 2 tablespoons (16 grams) tea, salt, baking soda, and remaining 3 cups (375 grams) flour. Add tea mixture to butter mixture alternately with buttermilk, beginning and ending with tea mixture, beating just until combined after each addition and stopping to scrape sides of bowl.

5. Spray a 12-cup Bundt pan with baking spray with flour. Spoon 3 cups (700 grams) batter into prepared pan. Tap pan on a kitchen towel-lined counter several times to settle batter and release any air bubbles. Using the back of a spoon, make a ¼- to ½-inch-deep, 1-inch-wide trench in center of batter in pan, leaving about a ¼- to ½-inch border around edges. Spoon half of remaining batter into a large pastry bag; cut a ½-inch opening in tip. Pipe a border of batter, tracing outer and inner edges of pan. Spoon cream cheese mixture and pipe batter in alternating dollops into trench in pan. After completing 1 ring in pan, pipe batter over cream cheese dollops and vice versa until cream cheese mixture is all used up. Drag a wooden pick through center of each dollop to swirl together. Pipe and gently spread remaining batter on top, covering cream cheese mixture. Do not tap pan.
6. Bake for 40 minutes. Rotate pan, and loosely cover with foil. Bake until a wooden pick inserted near center comes out clean and an instant-read thermometer inserted near center registers 205°F (96°C), 10 to 15 minutes more. Let cool in pan for 20 minutes. Using a small offset spatula, gently loosen cake from center of pan. Invert cake onto a wire rack placed over a rimmed baking sheet, and let cool completely.
7. Brush cooled cake with melted butter.
8. In a small bowl, whisk together remaining ⅓ cup (67 grams) granulated sugar and remaining 1 teaspoon (4 grams) tea. Cover cake with sugar mixture, pressing gently to help adhere. Serve immediately.

Note: *We used about 10 bags of Harney & Son's Earl Grey Tea, processing the contents with a spice grinder to yield about 2 tablespoons plus 1 teaspoon finely ground tea.*

SPICED PUMPKIN STREUSEL BUNDTLETTES

Makes 6 Bundtlettes

These adorable pumpkin mini cakes are a little sweet, a little spicy, and a little crunchy—and no sharing required.

Filling:

4	teaspoons (12 grams) all-purpose flour
4	teaspoons (20 grams) firmly packed light brown sugar
1½	teaspoons (3 grams) ground cinnamon*
¼	teaspoon pumpkin pie spice*
Pinch kosher salt	
1½	teaspoons (7.5 grams) unsalted butter, room temperature

Cake:

¾	cup plus 2 tablespoons (197 grams) canned pumpkin
½	cup plus 1 tablespoon (124 grams) firmly packed light brown sugar
⅓	cup (67 grams) granulated sugar
⅓	cup (75 grams) vegetable oil
⅓	cup (80 grams) crème fraîche, room temperature
1	large egg (50 grams), room temperature
1	large egg yolk (19 grams), room temperature
2	tablespoons (28 grams) unsalted butter, melted
1	teaspoon (6 grams) vanilla bean paste
1	cup (125 grams) all-purpose flour
1	teaspoon (5 grams) baking powder
¾	teaspoon (2.25 grams) kosher salt
¾	teaspoon (1.5 grams) ground nutmeg*
½	teaspoon (1 gram) pumpkin pie spice
¼	teaspoon (1.25 grams) baking soda
¼	teaspoon ground cinnamon

Cinnamon Glaze (recipe follows)
Garnish: ground cinnamon, roasted salted pumpkin seeds (pepitas)

1. Preheat oven to 325°F (170°C).
2. For filling: In a small bowl, stir together flour, brown sugar, cinnamon, pie spice, and salt. Add butter, and rub in by hand until mixture is sandy and well combined.
3. For cake: In a large bowl, whisk together pumpkin, brown sugar, granulated sugar, oil, crème fraîche, egg, egg yolk, melted butter, and vanilla bean paste.
4. In a medium bowl, whisk together flour, baking powder, salt, nutmeg, pie spice, baking soda, and cinnamon. Gradually whisk flour mixture into pumpkin mixture just until smooth and well combined.
5. Spray a 5-cup Bundtlette pan with baking spray with flour. Divide one-third of batter among prepared wells (about 2½ tablespoons or 40 grams each). Tap pan on a kitchen towel-lined counter a few times to settle batter and release any air bubbles. Using a small spoon, divide half of filling (about 2 tablespoons or 20 grams) among wells, leaving about a ¼-inch border around edges. (It's OK if some of filling touches edges of pan.) Top with one-third of batter; spread batter to cover filling. Tap pan on a kitchen towel-lined counter a few times to settle batter and release any air bubbles. Sprinkle with remaining filling; cover with remaining batter, spreading to cover filling. Tap on a kitchen towel-lined counter a few times to settle batter and release any air bubbles.
6. Bake until a wooden pick inserted near center comes out clean, 12 to 20 minutes. Let cool in pan for 15 minutes. Invert Bundtlettes onto a wire rack, and let cool completely.
7. Drizzle Cinnamon Glaze onto cooled cakes. Garnish with cinnamon and pumpkin seeds, if desired.

We used Simply Organic Ground Cinnamon, Simply Organic Pumpkin Pie Spice, and Simply Organic Ground Nutmeg.

CINNAMON GLAZE
Makes about ¾ cup

1¾	cups (210 grams) confectioners' sugar
2	tablespoons (30 grams) whole milk
1½	tablespoons (22.5 grams) crème fraîche
¼	teaspoon kosher salt
⅛	teaspoon ground cinnamon

1. In a medium bowl, whisk together all ingredients until smooth. Use immediately.

BOOZY
BAKES

RATHER THAN POURING YOUR POTENT
POTABLE INTO A GLASS, WE ENCOURAGE
YOU TO SPIKE YOUR CAKE INSTEAD

STRAWBERRY CHABLIS CAKE

Makes 1 (6-cup) cake

My wine of choice is Chablis, and strawberries pair beautifully with it, so I thought why not make a cake with them! Roasting the strawberries adds an intense, sweet note to the cake that's well worth the extra step. All that's needed is layer of vanilla-kissed cream and a scattering of fresh strawberries to top off this indulgent treat.

1	cup (165 grams) chopped fresh strawberries
¾	cup (150 grams) plus 2 tablespoons (24 grams) granulated sugar, divided
⅓	cup (75 grams) unsalted butter, softened
1	large egg (50 grams), room temperature
2	teaspoons (8 grams) vanilla extract, divided
1½	cups (188 grams) all-purpose flour
1½	teaspoons (7.5 grams) baking powder
½	teaspoon (1.5 grams) kosher salt
½	cup (120 grams) Chablis wine
1	cup (240 grams) cold heavy whipping cream
¼	cup (30 grams) confectioners' sugar

Garnish: fresh strawberries

1. Preheat oven to 350°F (180°C). Line a rimmed baking sheet with parchment paper.

2. In a medium bowl, toss together chopped strawberries and 2 tablespoons (24 grams) granulated sugar until combined. Spread in a single layer on prepared pan.

3. Bake until berries are soft and fragrant and juices begin to thicken at edges of pan, 15 to 20 minutes, stirring every 5 to 10 minutes. Let cool completely on pan. Leave oven on.

4. Strain cooled strawberries through a fine-mesh sieve.

5. In the bowl of a stand mixer fitted with the paddle attachment, beat butter and remaining ¾ cup (150 grams) granulated sugar at medium speed until light and fluffy, 2 to 4 minutes, stopping to scrape sides of bowl. Add egg and 1 teaspoon (4 grams) vanilla, beating well and stopping to scrape sides of bowl.

6. In a medium bowl, whisk together flour, baking powder, and salt. With mixer on low speed, gradually add flour mixture to butter mixture alternately with wine, beginning and ending with flour mixture, beating until just combined after each addition. Carefully fold in roasted strawberries.

7. Spray a Nordic Ware 6-Cup Charlotte Cake Pan with baking spray with flour. Pour batter into prepared pan, leveling as needed. Firmly tap pan on a kitchen towel-lined counter to settle batter.

8. Bake until a wooden pick inserted in center comes out with a few moist crumbs, 25 to 30 minutes. Let cool in pan for 10 minutes. Remove from pan, and let cool completely on a wire rack.

9. Clean bowl of stand mixer. Using the whisk attachment, beat cold cream, confectioners' sugar, and remaining 1 teaspoon (4 grams) vanilla at medium-high speed until stiff peaks form, 4 to 5 minutes. Cover and refrigerate until ready to serve.

10. When ready to serve, top cake with whipped cream mixture. Garnish with strawberries, if desired. Refrigerate in an airtight container for up to 3 days.

CIDER-SPIKED KENTUCKY BUTTER BUNDTLETTES

Makes 12 Bundtlettes

Recipe adapted from Cheryl Norris

For our fall take on the Kentucky butter cake, we swapped in crisp hard apple cider for the usual rum. Then, we transformed this Bundt cake into perfectly portioned Bundtlettes—doubling the sweet surface area for the delicious glaze.

1½	cups (340 grams) unsalted butter, softened and divided
3	cups (600 grams) granulated sugar, divided
4	large eggs (200 grams), room temperature
4	teaspoons (16 grams) vanilla extract, divided
3	cups (375 grams) all-purpose flour
1	teaspoon (5 grams) baking powder
1	teaspoon (3 grams) kosher salt
1	teaspoon (2 grams) ground cinnamon
½	teaspoon (2.5 grams) baking soda
½	teaspoon (1 gram) ground nutmeg
¼	teaspoon ground allspice
¾	cup (180 grams) whole buttermilk, room temperature
¾	cup (180 grams) hard apple cider, divided (see Notes)

1. Preheat oven to 325°F (170°C).

2. In the bowl of a stand mixer fitted with paddle attachment, beat 1 cup (227 grams) butter and 2 cups (400 grams) sugar at medium speed until fluffy, 3 to 4 minutes, stopping to scrape sides of bowl. Add eggs, one at a time, beating just until combined after each addition. Beat in 2 teaspoons (8 grams) vanilla.

3. In a large bowl, whisk together flour, baking powder, salt, cinnamon, baking soda, nutmeg, and allspice. In a small bowl, whisk together buttermilk and ½ cup (120 grams) cider. With mixer on low speed, gradually add flour mixture to butter mixture alternately with buttermilk mixture, beginning and ending with flour mixture, beating just until combined after each addition.

4. Spray 2 (5-cup) Bundtlette pans with baking spray with flour. Divide batter among prepared wells, filling about two-thirds full. (See Notes.)

5. Bake until a wooden pick inserted near center comes out clean, 20 to 25 minutes. Let cool in pans on wire racks for 10 minutes.

6. Meanwhile, in a small saucepan, melt remaining ½ cup (113 grams) butter over medium-low heat. Add remaining 1 cup (200 grams) sugar, remaining ¼ cup (60 grams) cider, and remaining 2 teaspoons (8 grams) vanilla. Cook, stirring frequently, until sugar dissolves, about 1 minute.

7. Poke warm cakes all over with a wooden pick. Evenly pour 1 cup (240 grams) warm glaze all over cakes. Let stand until glaze is completely absorbed, 10 to 15 minutes. Invert cakes onto wire racks. Brush tops and sides of cakes with remaining ½ cup (120 grams) warm glaze. Let cool completely.

Notes: *To make this nonalcoholic, use an equal amount of regular apple cider.*

If you have only 1 Bundtlette pan, you can halve the recipe.

BRANDIED APPLE SPICE CAKE

Makes 1 (6-cup) cake

This cake is filled with the best of fall: fragrant spices, crisp apples, and warming brandy, which keeps the cake incredibly moist and tender.

1¼   cups (156 grams) all-purpose flour
1½   teaspoons (3 grams) ground cinnamon
½   teaspoon (2.5 grams) baking powder
½   teaspoon (1.5 grams) kosher salt
½   teaspoon (1 gram) ground allspice
½   teaspoon (1 gram) ground nutmeg
¼   teaspoon (1.25 grams) baking soda
¼   teaspoon ground ginger
½   cup (120 grams) whole buttermilk, room temperature
¼   cup (56 grams) vegetable oil
2   large eggs (100 grams), room temperature
1   teaspoon (4 grams) vanilla extract
½   cup (100 grams) granulated sugar
¼   cup (55 grams) firmly packed light brown sugar
Brandy Syrup (recipe follows)
Apple Brandy Topping (recipe follows)

1. Preheat oven to 350°F (180°C).
2. In a medium bowl, whisk together flour, cinnamon, baking powder, salt, allspice, nutmeg, baking soda, and ginger.
3. In a large bowl, whisk together buttermilk, oil, eggs, and vanilla; stir in sugars. Add flour mixture, and whisk until just combined.
4. Spray a Nordic Ware 6-Cup Charlotte Cake Pan with baking spray with flour. Pour batter into prepared pan, leveling as needed. Firmly tap pan on a kitchen towel-lined counter to settle batter.
5. Bake until a wooden pick inserted in center comes out with a few moist crumbs, 25 to 30 minutes. Let cool in pan for 10 minutes. Remove from pan, and place on a wire rack. Using a pastry brush, lightly brush Brandy Syrup onto warm cake. (The more syrup you add, the stronger the alcohol flavor.) Let cool completely.
6. Top cooled cake with Apple Brandy Topping. Serve immediately. Refrigerate in an airtight container for up to 3 days.

BRANDY SYRUP

Makes about ¼ cup

¼   cup (50 grams) granulated sugar
¼   cup (60 grams) apple brandy

1. In a small saucepan, bring sugar and brandy to a boil over high heat, stirring frequently until sugar dissolves. Cook for 1 to 2 minutes.

APPLE BRANDY TOPPING

Makes about 3 cups

3   cups (375 grams) chopped peeled Honeycrisp or Gala apples, divided
½   cup (110 grams) firmly packed light brown sugar
½   teaspoon (1.5 grams) kosher salt
½   teaspoon (1 gram) ground cinnamon
2   teaspoons (10 grams) fresh lemon juice
½   teaspoon (2 grams) vanilla extract
¼   cup (57 grams) unsalted butter
3   tablespoons (45 grams) apple brandy*
2   tablespoons (30 grams) water
2   teaspoons (6 grams) cornstarch

1. In a medium bowl, combine 2 cups (250 grams) apples, brown sugar, salt, and cinnamon. Add lemon juice and vanilla.
2. In a medium saucepan, melt butter over medium heat. Add apple mixture and brandy, stirring until combined. Bring to a boil.
3. In a small bowl, whisk together 2 tablespoons (30 grams) water and cornstarch. Slowly add to apple mixture, stirring constantly. Add remaining 1 cup (125 grams) chopped apples. Return to a boil, and cook, stirring frequently, until thickened and translucent and apples are tender, about 3 minutes. Remove from heat, and let cool completely.

We used Calvados.

BERMUDA RUM CAKE

Makes 1 (10-cup) cake

Recipe courtesy of Kamilah Cannonier

Bermuda is one of my favorite island destinations, and I make sure to sample rum cake each time I'm there. You'll find variations of this dense, buttery bake throughout the island, but I'm partial to this recipe that local baker Kamilah Cannonier shared me. With just one bite, you'll almost feel the island breeze against your face and your toes sinking into the warm sand.

1	cup (227 grams) unsalted butter, softened
2	cups (400 grams) granulated sugar
4	large eggs (200 grams)
1	teaspoon (4 grams) vanilla extract
3	cups (375 grams) all-purpose flour
1	tablespoon (15 grams) baking powder
1	teaspoon (3 grams) kosher salt
¾	cup (180 grams) whole milk, room temperature
1¼	cups (300 grams) dark rum*, divided
1½	cups (180 grams) confectioners' sugar

1. Preheat oven to 350°F (180°C).

2. In the bowl of a stand mixer fitted with the paddle attachment, beat butter and granulated sugar at medium speed until fluffy, 4 to 5 minutes, stopping to scrape sides of bowl. Reduce mixer speed to low. Add eggs, one at a time, beating well after each addition. Beat in vanilla.

3. In a medium bowl, whisk together flour, baking powder, and salt. With mixer on low speed, gradually add flour mixture to butter mixture alternately with milk, beginning and ending with flour mixture, beating just until combined after each addition. Add ¼ cup (60 grams) rum; beat at medium speed until well combined.

4. Spray a 10-cup Bundt pan with baking spray with flour. Pour batter into prepared pan.

5. Bake until a wooden pick inserted near center comes out clean, 45 to 50 minutes. Using a wooden skewer, poke holes in hot cake. Slowly pour ⅓ cup (80 grams) rum all over cake. Let cool for 10 to 12 minutes. Invert cake onto a wire rack. Using a wooden skewer, poke holes in top of warm cake. Slowly pour ⅓ cup (80 grams) rum all over cake. Let cake cool completely.

6. In a small bowl, whisk together confectioners' sugar and remaining ⅓ cup (80 grams) rum; drizzle onto cake. Let stand for 5 minutes before serving.

*Kamilah uses Goslings Black Seal Bermuda Black Rum.

Note: *For a thicker glaze, whisk in additional confectioners' sugar, 1 tablespoon at a time, until desired consistency is reached.*

RED WINE CHOCOLATE CAKE WITH RASPBERRY GLAZE

Makes 1 (6-cup) cake

Baking with red wine is inspired; combined with chocolate and raspberries, we can't think of a more romantic combination that lingers on the palate.

½	cup (113 grams) unsalted butter, softened
1	cup (200 grams) granulated sugar
1	large egg (50 grams), room temperature
1	teaspoon (4 grams) vanilla extract
1	cup (125 grams) all-purpose flour
⅓	cup (25 grams) unsweetened cocoa powder
1	teaspoon (5 grams) baking powder
½	teaspoon (1.5 grams) kosher salt
¼	teaspoon (1.25 grams) baking soda
¾	cup (180 grams) dry red wine
1	cup (120 grams) confectioners' sugar
¼	cup (60 grams) heavy whipping cream
3	tablespoons (60 grams) seedless raspberry preserves

Garnish: chocolate curls

1. Preheat oven to 350°F (180°C).

2. In the bowl of a stand mixer fitted with the paddle attachment, beat butter and granulated sugar at medium speed until light and fluffy, 3 to 4 minutes, stopping to scrape sides of bowl. Add egg and vanilla, beating well and stopping to scrape sides of bowl.

3. In a medium bowl, whisk together flour, cocoa, baking powder, salt, and baking soda. With mixer on low speed, gradually add flour mixture to butter mixture alternately with wine, beginning and ending with flour mixture, beating until just combined after each addition.

4. Spray a Nordic Ware 6-Cup Charlotte Cake Pan with baking spray with flour. Pour batter into prepared pan. Firmly tap pan on a kitchen towel-lined counter to settle batter.

5. Bake until a wooden pick inserted in center comes out clean and an instant-read thermometer inserted in center registers 205°F (96°C), 30 to 45 minutes. Let cool in pan for 10 minutes. Remove from pan, and let cool completely on a wire rack.

6. In a small bowl, whisk together confectioners' sugar, cream, and preserves. Spoon on top of cooled cake. Garnish with chocolate curls, if desired. Refrigerate in an airtight container for up to 3 days.

HOLIDAY CLASSICS

GINGERBREAD, PEPPERMINT, AMBROSIA,
AND MORE TRADITIONAL FLAVORS
BAKED IN A BUNDT MAKE FOR A
FESTIVE CELEBRATORY SEASON

GERMAN CHOCOLATE BUNDT CAKE

Makes 1 (12-cup) Bundt cake

We've made a German Chocolate Bundt Cake recipe that is better than ever, with tender-crumbed chocolate cake sandwiching a thick and rich Coconut-Pecan Filling. The indulgent cake comes together with bold unsweetened cocoa powder and decadently sweet baking chocolate. The filling combines sweetened flaked coconut with earthy chopped pecans for a beautiful crunch in each bite. Need more chocolate? Cover it with our Creamy Chocolate Frosting final step to a picture-perfect masterpiece!

1   cup (227 grams) unsalted butter, softened
1   cup (200 grams) granulated sugar
1   cup (220 grams) firmly packed light brown sugar
4   large eggs (200 grams), room temperature
1   teaspoon (4 grams) vanilla extract
2½   cups (313 grams) all-purpose flour
¼   cup (21 grams) unsweetened cocoa powder
½   teaspoon (2.5 grams) baking powder
½   teaspoon (2.5 grams) baking soda
½   teaspoon (1.5 grams) kosher salt
1½   cups (360 grams) whole buttermilk, room temperature
6   ounces (175 grams) sweet baking chocolate*, melted and cooled
Coconut-Pecan Filling (recipe follows)
Creamy Chocolate Frosting (recipe follows)
Garnish: lightly toasted sweetened flaked coconut, finely chopped toasted pecans

1. Preheat oven to 350°F (180°C).
2. In the bowl of a stand mixer fitted with the paddle attachment, beat butter and sugars at medium speed until fluffy, 3 to 4 minutes, stopping to scrape sides of bowl. Add eggs, one at a time, beating well after each addition. Beat in vanilla.
3. In a medium bowl, whisk together flour, cocoa, baking powder, baking soda, and salt. With mixer on low speed, gradually add flour mixture to butter mixture alternately with buttermilk, beginning and ending with flour mixture, beating just until combined after each addition. Stir in melted chocolate until combined.
4. Spray a 12-cup Bundt pan with baking spray with flour. Spoon batter into prepared pan, and spread into an even layer. Tap pan

on a kitchen towel-lined counter several times to settle batter and release any air bubbles.
5. Bake until a wooden pick inserted near center comes out clean, 50 to 55 minutes. Let cool in pan for 15 minutes. Invert cake onto a wire rack, and let cool completely.
6. Measuring 1¼ inches from bottom of cake, cut cake in half horizontally using a large, serrated knife. Using a cake board or cake lifter, remove top half of cake; reserve. Spread Coconut-Pecan Filling evenly onto bottom half. Replace top half. Spread Creamy Chocolate Frosting on top of cake. Garnish with toasted coconut and chopped pecans, if desired. (Refrigerate for 30 minutes to set frosting for a cleaner cut, if desired.)

*We used Baker's German's Sweet Chocolate.

COCONUT-PECAN FILLING
Makes 2 cups

⅔   cup (133 grams) granulated sugar
⅔   cup (160 grams) evaporated milk
2   large egg yolks (38 grams)
¼   teaspoon kosher salt
⅓   cup (76 grams) unsalted butter, cubed and softened
1   cup (110 grams) packed sweetened flaked coconut
⅔   cup (69 grams) finely chopped pecans
1   teaspoon (4 grams) vanilla extract

1. In a medium saucepan, whisk together sugar, evaporated milk, egg yolks, and salt until smooth. Add butter, and cook over medium heat, whisking frequently, until butter is melted. Cook, whisking constantly, until mixture is thickened and coats the back of a spoon and an instant-read thermometer registers 200°F (93°C), about 5 minutes.
2. Remove from heat; stir in coconut, pecans, and vanilla. Pour into a heatproof bowl, and cover with plastic wrap, pressing wrap directly onto surface of filling to prevent a skin from forming. Refrigerate until thick and cold, at least 2 hours or up to 3 days.

CREAMY CHOCOLATE FROSTING
Makes 1½ cups

½   cup (113 grams) unsalted butter, softened
2   tablespoons (10 grams) unsweetened cocoa powder
2   cups (240 grams) confectioners' sugar
2½   tablespoons (38 grams) whole buttermilk

1. In a medium bowl, beat butter with a hand mixer fitted with beater attachments at medium speed until smooth and creamy, about 1 minute. Add cocoa; beat at low speed until combined. With mixer on low speed, add confectioners' sugar, about ½ cup (60 grams) at a time, alternately with buttermilk, about 1 tablespoon (15 grams) at a time, beating until combined. Increase mixer speed to medium, and beat until slightly thickened, about 1 minute. Use immediately.

AMBROSIA POUND CAKE

Makes 1 (15-cup) Bundt cake

We turned a classic Southern fruit salad into a delicious and jewel-toned holiday stunner.

1½   cups (340 grams) unsalted butter, softened
2¼   cups (450 grams) granulated sugar
1   tablespoon (9 grams) plus ½ teaspoon (2 grams) orange zest, divided
3   large eggs (150 grams), room temperature
2   teaspoons (8 grams) vanilla extract
½   teaspoon (2 grams) coconut extract
3   cups (375 grams) plus 1 tablespoon (8 grams) all-purpose flour, divided
1   teaspoon (3 grams) kosher salt
¼   teaspoon (1.25 grams) baking soda
1   cup (240 grams) sour cream, room temperature
½   cup (135 grams) crushed pineapple
¾   cup (85 grams) finely chopped pecans
¾   cup (67 grams) sweetened flaked coconut
¾   cup (128 grams) stemmed maraschino cherries, chopped and patted dry
1   cup (120 grams) confectioners' sugar
1   tablespoon plus 1 teaspoon (20 grams) whole milk
Garnish: sweetened flaked coconut

1. Preheat oven to 325°F (170°C).
2. In the bowl of a stand mixer fitted with the paddle attachment, beat butter, granulated sugar, and 1 tablespoon (9 grams) orange zest at medium speed until fluffy, 5 to 6 minutes, stopping to scrape sides of bowl. Add eggs, one at a time, beating well after each addition. Beat in extracts.
3. In a large bowl, whisk together 3 cups (375 grams) flour, salt, and baking soda. With mixer on low speed, gradually add flour mixture to butter mixture alternately with sour cream and pineapple, beginning and ending with flour mixture, beating just until combined after each addition. Fold in pecans and coconut.
4. In a small bowl, toss together cherries and remaining 1 tablespoon (8 grams) flour; fold into batter.
5. Spray a 15-cup Bundt pan with baking spray with flour. Spoon batter into prepared pan. Tap pan on a kitchen towel-lined counter several times to settle batter and release any air bubbles.
6. Bake until a wooden pick inserted near center comes out with a few moist crumbs, about 1 hour and 25 minutes. Let cool in pan for 15 minutes. Invert cake onto a wire rack, and let cool completely.
7. In a small bowl, whisk together confectioners' sugar, milk, and remaining ½ teaspoon (2 grams) orange zest until smooth; pour onto cooled cake. Garnish with coconut, if desired. Store in an airtight container for up to 2 days.

VANILLA-PEPPERMINT SWIRL BUNDT CAKE

Makes 1 (10-cup) Bundt cake

Like the swirls of a candy cane, this red-hued beauty holds a magical surprise in its center. To create the magnificently marbled interior of this Bundt, one base batter is split into two and then layered one upon the other, with one colored red and brightly flavored with peppermint extract and the other delicately flavored with vanilla. The resulting cake is moist and tender, not to mention incredibly festive in flavor.

1⅓   cups (303 grams) unsalted butter, softened
2   cups (400 grams) granulated sugar
⅓   cup (73 grams) firmly packed light brown sugar
5   large eggs (250 grams), room temperature
1   large egg yolk (19 grams), room temperature
2⅔   cups (333 grams) all-purpose flour
1¼   teaspoons (3.75 grams) kosher salt
½   teaspoon (2.5 grams) baking powder
½   cup (120 grams) plus 1 teaspoon (5 grams) room temperature water, divided
⅓   cup (80 grams) sour cream, room temperature
4   teaspoons (8 grams) unsweetened cocoa powder, sifted
2½   teaspoons (12.5 grams) red liquid food coloring*
¾   teaspoon (3 grams) peppermint extract
1   teaspoon (6 grams) vanilla bean paste
Garnish: finely crushed soft peppermint candies (see Notes)

1. Preheat oven to 325°F (170°C).
2. In the bowl of a stand mixer fitted with the paddle attachment, beat butter and sugars at medium-low speed just until combined. Increase mixer speed to medium, and beat until fluffy, 4 to 5 minutes, stopping to scrape sides of bowl. Add eggs and egg yolk, one at a time, beating well after each addition.
3. In a medium bowl, whisk together flour, salt, and baking powder. In a small bowl, whisk together ½ cup (120 grams) room temperature water and sour cream. With mixer on low speed, gradually add flour mixture to butter mixture alternately with sour cream mixture, beginning and ending with flour mixture, beating just until combined after each addition. Transfer half of batter (about 3½ cups or 770 grams) to another medium bowl; fold in cocoa, food coloring, and peppermint extract until well combined. Fold vanilla bean paste and remaining 1 teaspoon (5 grams) room temperature water into remaining batter until well combined.
4. Spray a 10-cup Bundt pan with baking spray with flour. Dollop and gently spread one-third of red batter (about 1 cup or 257 grams) in bottom of prepared pan; top with one-third of vanilla batter (about 1 cup or 257 grams), dolloping and then gently spreading to edges of pan in an even layer. (It's OK if it's not perfect; if batters start to smudge together, wipe your utensil clean and continue spreading.) Repeat procedure twice until all batter is used. Firmly tap pan on a kitchen towel-lined counter several times to settle batter and release any air bubbles.
5. Bake for 50 minutes. Rotate pan, and bake until a wooden pick inserted near center comes out clean, crack in top of cake appears mostly dry, and an instant-read thermometer inserted near center registers 205°F (96°C) to 210°F (99°C), 12 to 20 minutes more. Let cool in pan for 15 minutes. Invert pan onto a wire rack. Gently tap wire rack on counter a few times to help loosen cake; remove pan, and let cake cool completely. Using a small fine-mesh sieve, dust with candies, if desired.

*We used McCormick Red Food Color.

Notes: *To finely crush candy, place in a small resealable plastic bag. Use a rolling pin to pound and crush candy until finely ground.*

This Bundt cake may have a small soft spot at the bottom where the warm cake crumbs get compressed when turned out onto the wire rack.

bake it a **BUNDT**LETTE

VANILLA-PEPPERMINT SWIRL BUNDTLETTES

Makes 6 Bundtlettes

⅔ cup (150 grams) unsalted butter, softened
1 cup (200 grams) granulated sugar
2½ tablespoons (35 grams) firmly packed light brown sugar
2 large eggs (100 grams), room temperature
2 large egg yolks (37 grams), room temperature
1⅓ cups (167 grams) all-purpose flour
½ teaspoon (1.5 grams) kosher salt
¼ teaspoon (1.25 grams) baking powder
¼ cup (60 grams) plus ½ teaspoon (2.5 grams) room temperature water, divided
3 tablespoons (45 grams) sour cream, room temperature
2 teaspoons (4 grams) unsweetened cocoa powder, sifted
1¼ teaspoons (6.25 grams) red liquid food coloring*
¼ teaspoon (1 gram) peppermint extract
½ teaspoon (3 grams) vanilla bean paste
Garnish: finely crushed soft peppermint candies (see Notes)

1. Preheat oven to 325°F (170°C).
2. In the bowl of a stand mixer fitted with the paddle attachment, beat butter and sugars at medium-low speed just until combined. Increase mixer speed to medium, and beat until fluffy, 4 to 5 minutes, stopping to scrape sides of bowl. Add eggs and egg yolks, one at a time, beating well after each addition.
3. In a medium bowl, whisk together flour, salt, and baking powder. In a small bowl, whisk together ¼ cup (60 grams) room temperature water and sour cream. With mixer on low speed, gradually add flour mixture to butter mixture alternately with sour cream mixture, beginning and ending with flour mixture, beating just until combined after each addition. Transfer half of batter (1⅓ to 1⅔ cups or about 384 grams) to another medium bowl; fold in cocoa, food coloring, and peppermint extract until well combined. Fold vanilla bean paste and remaining ½ teaspoon (2.5 grams) room temperature water into remaining batter until well combined.
4. Spray a 5-cup Bundtlette pan with baking spray with flour. Divide one-third of red batter among prepared wells, dolloping and spreading in an even layer (about 1 tablespoon or 18 grams per well); top with one-third of vanilla batter, dolloping and spreading in an even layer (about 1 tablespoon or 18 grams per well). (It's OK if it's not perfect; if batters start to smudge together, wipe your utensil clean and continue spreading.) Repeat procedure twice until all batter is used. Vigorously tap pan on a kitchen towel-lined counter several times to settle batter and release any air bubbles.
5. Bake until a wooden pick inserted near center comes out clean, 18 to 24 minutes. Let cool in pan for 15 minutes. Invert cakes onto a wire rack, and let cool completely. Using a small fine-mesh sieve, dust with candies, if desired.

*We used McCormick Red Food Color.

Notes: *To finely crush candy, place in a small resealable plastic bag. Use a rolling pin to pound and crush candy until finely ground.*

These Bundtlettes may have a small soft spot at the bottom where the warm cake crumbs get compressed when turned out onto the wire rack.

This Bundt's tighter, pound cake-like crumb bakes beautifully into the Let It Snow Bundt® Pan's intricate design, making for crisp details and a showstopping, festive result.

We dusted our cake with finely crushed soft peppermint candies for a snowy finish that highlights the pan's wintry aesthetic. Feel free to substitute confectioners' sugar if desired.

Arranging the two batters in alternating layers gives each slice candy cane-inspired stripes. We found the back of a small spoon makes for a great spreading tool. If the batters start to smudge while working, wipe your utensil clean and keep going.

More than just a flavoring, a touch of cocoa helps our red peppermint batter achieve its deep ruby hue.

Peppermint extract and vanilla bean paste give this cake a beautifully balanced holiday flavor. In general, peppermint extract is stronger than its vanilla counterparts, so start small and increase gradually when adding to recipes. Vanilla bean paste is a tad more pungent than vanilla extract and boasts beautiful seed flecks. That said, you can substitute both 1:1.

LANE CAKE

Makes 1 (6-cup) cake

The Alabama-born Lane Cake is one of my favorite holiday cakes, but it can be quite a process to bake and assemble the traditional layered version. With this bourbon-infused one-layer beauty, you get all the classic flavors and ingredients, but in a fraction of the time and with a fraction of the effort.

¾ cup (170 grams) unsalted butter, softened
1 cup (200 grams) granulated sugar
2 large egg whites (60 grams), room temperature
2 teaspoons (8 grams) vanilla extract
1½ cups (188 grams) all-purpose flour
¾ teaspoon (3.75 grams) baking powder
¾ teaspoon (2.25 grams) kosher salt
¼ teaspoon (1.25 grams) baking soda
½ cup (120 grams) whole buttermilk, room temperature
Lane Cake Topping (recipe follows)
Lane Cake Meringue (recipe follows)

1. Preheat oven to 350°F (180°C).
2. In the bowl of a stand mixer fitted with the paddle attachment, beat butter and sugar at medium speed until light and fluffy, 2 to 3 minutes. Add egg whites, one at a time, beating well after each addition. Beat in vanilla.
3. In a medium bowl, whisk together flour, baking powder, salt, and baking soda. With mixer on low speed, gradually add flour mixture to butter mixture alternately with buttermilk, beginning and ending with flour mixture, beating until just combined after each addition.
4. Spray a Nordic Ware 6-Cup Charlotte Cake Pan with baking spray with flour. Pour batter into prepared pan. Firmly tap pan on a kitchen towel-lined counter to settle batter.
5. Bake until a wooden pick inserted in center comes out clean, 30 to 45 minutes. Let cool in pan for 10 minutes. Remove from pan, and let cool completely on a wire rack.
6. Spoon Lane Cake Topping onto cooled cake.
7. Place Lane Cake Meringue in a pastry bag fitted with a ⁷⁄₁₆-inch French star piping tip (Ateco #864); pipe around border of cake as desired. Using a handheld kitchen torch, carefully brown meringue as desired. Serve immediately.

LANE CAKE TOPPING
Makes about 2 cups

¾ cup (85 grams) chopped pecans
¼ cup (57 grams) unsalted butter
½ cup (100 grams) granulated sugar
4 large egg yolks (74 grams), room temperature
½ cup (30 grams) sweetened flaked coconut
¼ cup (32 grams) golden raisins
¼ cup (32 grams) raisins
3 tablespoons (45 grams) bourbon

1. In a medium saucepan, cook pecans and butter over medium heat until butter is melted. Stir in sugar until combined. Stir in egg yolks until combined; cook, stirring occasionally, until mixture is very thick, 3 to 4 minutes. Remove from heat. Stir in coconut, all raisins, and bourbon. Let cool for 5 minutes; use immediately.

LANE CAKE MERINGUE
Makes about 2 cups

½ cup (100 grams) granulated sugar
2 large egg whites (60 grams)
¼ teaspoon kosher salt

1. In the heatproof bowl of a stand mixer, whisk together all ingredients by hand. Place bowl over a saucepan of simmering water. Cook, whisking frequently, until sugar completely dissolves and an instant-read thermometer registers 160°F (71°C).
2. Carefully return bowl to stand mixer. Using the whisk attachment, beat at high speed until stiff peaks form and bowl is cool to the touch, 2 to 3 minutes. Use immediately.

VANILLA BEAN-GLAZED GINGERBREAD BUNDT

Makes 1 (10-cup) Bundt cake

This decorative Bundt takes all the beloved spices of a gingerbread cookie and incorporates them into a delightfully rich and dense pound cake. Topped with a vanilla glaze and baked in the Nordic Ware Let It Snow Bundt Pan, this stunning cake is sure to get everyone in a festive spirit!

1½	cups (340 grams) unsalted butter, softened
2	cups (440 grams) firmly packed dark brown sugar
6	large eggs (300 grams), room temperature
⅓	cup (113 grams) unsulphured molasses
2	teaspoons (8 grams) vanilla extract
3	cups (375 grams) all-purpose flour
1½	tablespoons (9 grams) ground ginger
1	tablespoon (6 grams) ground cinnamon
1	tablespoon (6 grams) ground nutmeg
1	teaspoon (3 grams) kosher salt
1	teaspoon (2 grams) ground cloves
1	teaspoon (2 grams) ground allspice
½	teaspoon (2.5 grams) baking powder
1	cup (240 grams) whole milk, room temperature

Vanilla Bean Glaze (recipe follows)

1. Preheat oven to 350°F (180°C).

2. In the bowl of a stand mixer fitted with the paddle attachment, beat butter and brown sugar at medium speed until light and fluffy, 3 to 4 minutes, stopping to scrape sides of bowl. Add eggs, one at a time, beating until well combined after each addition. Beat in molasses and vanilla until well combined, stopping to scrape sides of bowl.

3. In a large bowl, whisk together flour, ginger, cinnamon, nutmeg, salt, cloves, allspice, and baking powder. With mixer on low speed, gradually add flour mixture to butter mixture alternately with milk, beginning and ending with flour mixture, beating just until combined after each addition. (Batter may look slightly broken at this point but will bake fine.)

4. Spray a 10-cup Bundt pan with baking spray with flour. Spoon batter into prepared pan. Firmly tap pan on a kitchen towel-lined counter 5 to 6 times to settle batter and release any air bubbles.

5. Bake until golden brown, a wooden pick inserted near center comes out clean, and an instant-read thermometer inserted near center registers 200°F (93°C), 1 hour to 1 hour and 5 minutes. Let cool in pan for 10 minutes. Invert cake onto a wire rack, and let cool completely.

6. Trim bottom of cooled cake, if desired. Transfer to a serving plate. Pour Vanilla Bean Glaze on top of cake; using a spoon, spread glaze to help evenly coat cake.

Vanilla Bean Glaze

Makes about 1½ cups

3	cups (360 grams) confectioners' sugar
⅓	cup (80 grams) whole milk, room temperature
2½	tablespoons (52.5 grams) light corn syrup
1½	teaspoons (9 grams) vanilla bean paste
½	teaspoon (1.5 grams) kosher salt

1. In a medium bowl, whisk together all ingredients until smooth and well combined. Use immediately.

CANDIED CHESTNUT-PECAN CAKE

Makes 1 (12- to 15-cup) Bundt cake

I've long been a fan of marrons glacé, or candied chestnuts, that are big in France but not well known in the United States. I'm on a mission to introduce them to everyone, and there's no better place to start than with this glistening cake.

Browned butter:
¾ cup (170 grams) unsalted butter

Topping:
1 cup (244 grams) quartered candied chestnuts*
¾ cup (85 grams) chopped pecans*
¾ cup (75 grams) chopped Honeycrisp apple
½ cup (110 grams) firmly packed light brown sugar
½ cup (113 grams) unsalted butter, melted

Batter:
1¾ cups (350 grams) granulated sugar
3 large eggs (150 grams), room temperature
1 tablespoon (18 grams) vanilla bean paste
2⅓ cups (292 grams) cake flour
1 teaspoon (5 grams) baking soda
¾ teaspoon (2.25 grams) kosher salt
½ teaspoon (1 gram) ground nutmeg
¾ cup (180 grams) full-fat Greek yogurt, room temperature

1. For browned butter: In a medium saucepan, melt butter over medium heat. Cook until butter turns a medium-brown color and has a nutty aroma, about 10 minutes. Transfer to a heatproof bowl, and refrigerate until solidified, about 1 hour. (See Note.)

2. Preheat oven to 325°F (170°C). Spray a 12- to 15-cup Bundt or tube pan with baking spray with flour.

3. For topping: In a medium bowl, stir together chestnuts, pecans, apple, brown sugar, and melted butter until well combined. Press firmly into bottom of prepared pan.

4. For batter: In the bowl of a stand mixer fitted with the paddle attachment, beat browned butter and granulated sugar at medium speed until fluffy, 3 to 4 minutes, stopping to scrape sides of bowl. Add eggs, one at a time, beating well after each addition. Beat in vanilla bean paste.

5. In another medium bowl, whisk together flour, baking soda, salt, and nutmeg. With mixer on low speed, add flour mixture to butter mixture in three additions alternately with yogurt, beginning and ending with flour mixture, beating just until combined after each addition.

6. Spoon batter into prepared pan, and spread into an even layer. Tap pan on a kitchen towel-lined counter several times to settle batter and release any air bubbles.

7. Bake until golden and a wooden pick inserted near center of cake comes out clean, 50 minutes to 1 hour. Let cool in pan for 10 minutes. Invert cake onto a wire rack set on a parchment paper-lined rimmed baking sheet. Let cool completely.

*We used Rex Marron Glacé with Syrup, available at amazon.com, and Schermer Pecans.

Note: *You should end up with about 137 grams browned butter. If you refrigerate your butter for longer than 1 hour, you may need to soften it before mixing with the sugar.*

CRANBERRY-ORANGE BUNDT CAKE

Makes 1 (10-cup) Bundt cake

Studded with ruby-red cranberries and sweet orange zest, this festive bake is everything you're looking for in a holiday cake.

1   cup (227 grams) unsalted butter, softened
1½   cups (300 grams) granulated sugar
2   teaspoons (10 grams) tightly packed orange zest, divided
3   large eggs (150 grams), room temperature
2   teaspoons (8 grams) vanilla extract
1   teaspoon (4 grams) almond extract
2   cups (250 grams) plus 2 tablespoons (16 grams) all-purpose flour, divided
½   teaspoon (1.5 grams) kosher salt
¼   teaspoon (1.25 grams) baking soda
⅓   cup (80 grams) whole buttermilk, room temperature
2   cups (245 grams) fresh or thawed frozen cranberries
2   cups (240 grams) confectioners' sugar
3   tablespoons (45 grams) fresh orange juice

1. Preheat oven to 325°F (170°C).
2. In the bowl of a stand mixer fitted with the paddle attachment, beat butter, granulated sugar, and 1 teaspoon (5 grams) orange zest at medium speed until fluffy, 3 to 4 minutes, stopping to scrape sides of bowl. Add eggs, one at a time, beating well after each addition. Beat in extracts.
3. In a medium bowl, whisk together 2 cups (250 grams) flour, salt, and baking soda. With mixer on low speed, gradually add flour mixture to butter mixture alternately with buttermilk, beginning and ending with flour mixture, beating just until combined after each addition.
4. In a small bowl, toss together cranberries and remaining 2 tablespoons (16 grams) flour. Fold cranberries into batter.
5. Spray a 10-cup Bundt pan with baking spray with flour. Spoon batter into prepared pan. Gently tap pan on a kitchen towel-lined counter several times to settle batter and release any air bubbles.
6. Bake until a wooden pick inserted near center comes out clean, about 1 hour. Let cool in pan for 15 minutes. Invert cake onto a wire rack, and let cool completely.
7. In a small bowl, whisk together confectioners' sugar, orange juice, and remaining 1 teaspoon (5 grams) orange zest until smooth. Pour onto cooled cake.

GINGERBREAD STREUSEL BUNDT CAKE

Makes 1 (10-cup) Bundt cake

To make this delectable treat, a batter baked with molasses and holiday spices is layered with a double dose of streusel. Our cozy cake is sweetened with dark brown sugar, softly accented with almond extract, and highlighted with citrusy orange zest, and the streusel is made with bright flavors of ginger and orange zest for a wintry surprise in each bite. With a holiday pairing like this, our cake is destined to be the center of attention during your season of cheer.

¾ cup (170 grams) unsalted butter, softened
1⅓ cups (293 grams) firmly packed dark brown sugar
3 large eggs (150 grams), room temperature
½ cup (170 grams) unsulphured molasses
1 tablespoon (7 grams) tightly packed orange zest
½ teaspoon (2 grams) almond extract
2½ cups (313 grams) all-purpose flour
2 teaspoons (4 grams) ground ginger
2 teaspoons (4 grams) ground cinnamon
1½ teaspoons (3 grams) ground nutmeg
¾ teaspoon (2.25 grams) kosher salt
½ teaspoon (2.5 grams) baking powder
½ teaspoon (2.5 grams) baking soda
½ teaspoon (2 grams) ground cloves
½ teaspoon (2 grams) ground allspice
½ cup (120 grams) whole buttermilk, room temperature
Spiced Streusel (recipe follows)
Garnish: confectioners' sugar

1. Preheat oven to 350°F (180°C).
2. In the bowl of a stand mixer fitted with the paddle attachment, beat butter and brown sugar at medium speed until light and fluffy, 3 to 4 minutes, stopping to scrape sides of bowl. Add eggs, one at a time, beating until well combined after each addition. Beat in molasses, orange zest, and almond extract until well combined, stopping to scrape sides of bowl.
3. In a large bowl, whisk together flour, ginger, cinnamon, nutmeg, salt, baking powder, baking soda, cloves, and allspice. With mixer on low speed, gradually add flour mixture to butter mixture alternately with buttermilk, beginning and ending with flour mixture, beating just until combined after each addition. (Batter may have a little texture.)

4. Spray a 10-cup Bundt pan with baking spray with flour. Spoon two-thirds of batter (about 3½ cups or 808 grams) into prepared pan. Firmly tap pan on a kitchen towel-lined counter 5 to 6 times to settle batter and release any air bubbles. Using the back of a spoon, make a ½-inch-deep, 1-inch-wide trench in center of batter in pan, leaving about a ¼-inch border around edges. Sprinkle ⅔ cup (88 grams) Spiced Streusel in trench, making sure it does not touch sides of pan. Lightly press on streusel to make sure it is even and flat. Spoon remaining batter on top of streusel in pan in small dollops. Firmly tap pan on a kitchen towel-lined counter 5 to 6 times to settle batter and release any air bubbles. (Batter might pop as air is released from streusel filling.) Sprinkle remaining Spiced Streusel onto batter, trying not to touch sides of pan.
5. Bake until golden brown, a wooden pick inserted near center comes out clean, and an instant-read thermometer inserted near center registers 200°F (93°C), 45 minutes to 55 minutes. Let cool in pan for 15 minutes. Invert cake onto a wire rack, and let cool completely. Garnish with confectioners' sugar before serving, if desired.

SPICED STREUSEL
Makes about 1½ cups

½ cup (63 grams) all-purpose flour
½ cup (100 grams) granulated sugar
2 teaspoons (5 grams) tightly packed orange zest
1 teaspoon (2 grams) ground cinnamon
¼ teaspoon kosher salt
⅛ teaspoon ground ginger
3 tablespoons (42 grams) cold unsalted butter, cubed

1. In a medium bowl, whisk together flour, sugar, orange zest, cinnamon, salt, and ginger. Using your fingertips, work cold butter into flour mixture until no large chunks remain. Squeeze mixture and crumble until uniform in texture. (Mixture will look sandy.) Refrigerate until ready to use.

CLASSIC HUMMINGBIRD CAKE

Makes 1 (6-cup) cake

Swathed in a thick layer of decadent frosting, this fruit-filled spice cake tastes even better the day after it's baked. I love it!

1¾   cups (219 grams) all-purpose flour
½   cup (100 grams) granulated sugar
½   cup (110 grams) firmly packed light brown sugar
¾   teaspoon (1.5 grams) ground cinnamon
½   teaspoon (2.5 grams) baking soda
¼   teaspoon kosher salt
¼   teaspoon ground nutmeg
1   (8-ounce) can (227 grams) crushed pineapple, drained
⅔   cup (160 grams) mashed ripe banana (about 2 medium bananas)
½   cup (112 grams) neutral oil
1   large egg (50 grams), room temperature
1   teaspoon (4 grams) vanilla extract
½   cup (52 grams) finely chopped toasted pecans
Cream Cheese Frosting (recipe follows)
Garnish: finely chopped toasted pecans

1. Preheat oven to 350°F (180°C).
2. In a large bowl, whisk together flour, sugars, cinnamon, baking soda, salt, and nutmeg.
3. In a medium bowl, whisk together pineapple, banana, oil, egg, and vanilla. Add pineapple mixture to flour mixture, whisking just until combined. Fold in pecans.
4. Spray a Nordic Ware 6-Cup Charlotte Cake Pan with baking spray with flour. Pour batter into prepared pan. Tap pan on a kitchen towel-lined counter several times to settle batter and release any air bubbles.
5. Bake until a wooden pick inserted in center comes out clean, 45 to 50 minutes. Let cool in pan for 10 minutes. Remove from pan, and let cool completely on a wire rack.
6. Place Cream Cheese Frosting in a pastry bag fitted with a ½-inch French star piping tip (Ateco #865). Pipe on top of cake as desired. Garnish with pecans, if desired. Refrigerate until frosting is set, 15 to 20 minutes, if desired. Cover and refrigerate for up to 3 days.

CREAM CHEESE FROSTING

Makes about 2 cups

6   ounces (170 grams) cream cheese, softened
¼   cup (57 grams) unsalted butter, softened
2¾   cups (330 grams) confectioners' sugar

1. In a medium bowl, beat cream cheese and butter with a hand mixer fitted with beater attachments at medium speed until creamy, about 1 minute. Gradually add confectioners' sugar, beating until combined and stopping to scrape sides of bowl. Increase mixer speed to medium-high, and beat until slightly thickened, about 1 minute. Use immediately.

CHOCOLATE-ALMOND OLIVE OIL CAKE

Makes 1 (10-cup) Bundt cake

Baked in the glorious Star of David Bundt Pan and carrying the flavors of the crunchy mandelbrot *cookie, this tender dessert combines two Jewish traditions into one beautiful cake. Akin to the biscotti, Jewish* mandelbrot *or mandel bread is a twice-baked cookie made with neutral oil, chocolate chips, and almonds. Our Bundt version features the signature flavors as well as spices and citrus zest.*

3   large eggs (150 grams), room temperature
1½ cups (300 grams) granulated sugar
¾   cup (168 grams) extra-virgin olive oil
½   cup (120 grams) water or whole milk, room temperature
1   tablespoon (13 grams) vanilla extract
2   teaspoons (6 grams) tightly packed mandarin zest
2   cups (250 grams) all-purpose flour
1   cup (96 grams) blanched almond flour
2   teaspoons (10 grams) baking powder
1   teaspoon (3 grams) kosher salt
1   teaspoon (2 grams) ground cinnamon
½   teaspoon (1 gram) ground cloves
¾   cup (120 grams) chopped 64% cacao semisweet chocolate
Garnish: confectioners' sugar

1. Preheat oven to 350°F (180°C).
2. In the bowl of a stand mixer fitted with the whisk attachment, beat eggs at high speed until uniform in color and foamy, about 1 minute. With mixer on medium speed, add granulated sugar in a slow, steady stream. Increase mixer speed to high, and beat until thick and pale, about 2 minutes. With mixer on medium-high speed, add oil in a slow, steady stream, beating until combined; scrape sides of bowl. With mixer on medium speed, add ½ cup (120 grams) water or milk in a slow, steady stream, beating until combined. Beat in vanilla and mandarin zest.
3. In a medium bowl, whisk together flours, baking powder, salt, cinnamon, and cloves. Add flour mixture to egg mixture in two additions, folding with a balloon whisk just until combined after each addition. Fold in chocolate.
4. Spray a 10-cup Bundt pan with baking spray with flour. Pour batter into prepared pan. Tap pan on a kitchen towel-lined counter 5 to 6 times.
5. Bake until a wooden pick inserted near center comes out clean, 45 to 50 minutes, covering with foil after 25 minutes of baking to prevent excess browning. Let cool in pan for 10 minutes. Invert cake onto a wire rack, and let cool completely. Garnish with confectioners' sugar, if desired.

THE SIGNIFICANCE OF OIL

Hanukkah celebrates the endurance and tenacity of the Jewish faith, commemorating the reclaiming of Jerusalem from the despotic reign of King Antiochus in 165 BC and the rededication of the sacred Second Temple. Upon entering the Temple, the Jewish army found it in ruins and the eternal light snuffed out. One precious cask of pure oil was found, only enough to relight the flame for one day. However, miraculously, the flame burned for eight days and nights, allowing the soldiers enough time to prepare the Temple and rededicate it to the Jewish people. Since then, food made with and fried in oil, like latkes, *sufganiyot*, and mandelbrot, are served during Hanukkah in remembrance of that miraculous substance.

SAVORY & YEASTED

BOLD FLAVORS THAT RISE HIGH

SQUASH-SAGE PULL-APART BREAD

Makes 1 (12-cup) loaf

The pillowy, amber-hued dough is infused with roasted butternut squash and fresh sage for an earthy, mildly sweet flavor. After its first rise, each ball of dough is dipped in a browned butter-sage mixture and drizzled with any that's left over, resulting in a nutty, savory Bundt perfect for sharing.

3 to 3¼ cups (375 to 406 grams) all-purpose flour, divided
¼ cup (50 grams) granulated sugar
3½ teaspoons (10.5 grams) kosher salt (see Notes) divided
2¼ teaspoons (7 grams) instant yeast
1 teaspoon (2 grams) onion powder, divided
½ cup (120 grams) water
¼ cup (60 grams) whole milk
8 tablespoons (112 grams) unsalted butter, softened and divided
⅔ cup (162 grams) butternut squash purée (see Notes)
2½ teaspoons (3 grams) chopped fresh sage
4 (2½- to 2¾-inch-long) fresh sage leaves
Garnish: freshly shredded Parmesan cheese

1. In the bowl of a stand mixer fitted with the paddle attachment, beat 1 cup (125 grams) flour, sugar, 2¾ teaspoons (8.25 grams) salt, yeast, and ½ teaspoon (1 gram) onion powder at low speed until combined.
2. In a small saucepan, heat ½ cup (120 grams) water, milk, and 2 tablespoons (28 grams) butter over medium heat, stirring occasionally, until butter is melted and an instant-read thermometer registers 120°F (49°C) to 130°F (54°C). Add warm milk mixture to flour mixture; beat at medium speed for 1 minute, stopping to scrape sides of bowl. Add squash; beat just until combined, about 30 seconds. With mixer on low speed, gradually add 2 cups (250 grams) flour and chopped sage, beating just until combined.
3. Switch to the dough hook attachment. Beat at low speed until dough is soft and somewhat sticky and mostly clears sides of bowl, 8 to 12 minutes, stopping to scrape sides of bowl and dough hook; add up to remaining ¼ cup (31 grams) flour, 1 tablespoon (8 grams) at a time, if dough is too sticky. (Dough should pass the windowpane test; see Notes.) Turn out onto a lightly floured surface, and shape into a ball.
4. Spray a large bowl with cooking spray. Place dough in bowl, turning to grease top. Cover and let rise in a warm, draft-free place (75°F/24°C) until doubled in size, 50 minutes to 1 hour.

5. In a small saucepan, heat remaining 6 tablespoons (84 grams) butter over medium heat until melted and bubbling. Add sage leaves; cook, stirring occasionally, until leaves are slightly crisp and butter solids are light amber in color and nutty in aroma, 3 to 6 minutes. Transfer butter mixture to a small heatproof bowl; let cool for 15 minutes. (Butter should be just warm to the touch.) Discard sage. Stir in remaining ¾ teaspoon (2.25 grams) salt and remaining ½ teaspoon (1 gram) onion powder.
6. Spray a 12-cup Bundt pan with baking spray with flour.
7. Punch down dough; let stand for 10 minutes. On a clean surface, divide dough into 30 portions (26 to 28 grams each); gently shape each portion into a ball, pinching closed any seams, if needed. (Keep dough portions covered with a sheet of plastic wrap while working.) Dip dough balls in butter mixture, turning until well coated and letting excess drip off; arrange evenly in prepared pan, firmly pressing dough balls into each other and grooves of pan. Pour and spread remaining butter mixture over top of dough; firmly press dough balls into an even layer in pan. Cover and let rise in a warm, draft-free place (75°F/24°C) until puffed and dough holds an indentation when pressed, 25 to 35 minutes.
8. Preheat oven to 350°F (180°C).
9. Bake until top is golden brown and an instant-read thermometer inserted near center registers 195°F (88°C) to 210°F (98°C), 17 to 22 minutes. Let cool in pan for 5 minutes; invert loaf onto a serving plate. Garnish with cheese, if desired. Serve immediately.

Notes: *We used Diamond Crystal Kosher Salt, which has a different grain shape and a lighter, less salty flavor than coarser kosher salts. If measuring by volume, use half the amount of coarse kosher salt (such as Morton's). Especially for breads, though, it's often safest to measure salt by weight for the most consistent results.*

To make butternut squash purée, halve and seed a medium butternut squash and then coat it on all sides with 1 tablespoon (14 grams) vegetable oil. Bake, cut side down, on a parchment paper-lined baking sheet at 375°F (190°C) until very fork-tender, 50 minutes to 1 hour. Let cool completely on pan. For best color, trim and discard any browned spots. Scoop squash into the work bowl of a food processor and pulse until mostly smooth, stopping to scrape sides of bowl. (Alternatively, mash using a potato masher.) Reserve any extra squash purée for another use.

Test the dough for proper gluten development using the windowpane test. Pinch off (don't tear) a small piece of dough, lightly flouring hands if necessary. Slowly pull the dough out from the center. If the dough is ready, you will be able to stretch it until it's thin and translucent like a windowpane. If the dough tears, it's not quite ready. Beat for 1 minute, and test again.

bake it a **BUNDT**LETTE

MINI SQUASH-SAGE PULL-APART BREADS

Makes 6 Bundtlettes

1 to 1¼ cups (126 to 157 grams) all-purpose flour, divided
4   teaspoons (16 grams) granulated sugar
1   teaspoon (2.25 grams) kosher salt (see Notes) divided
¾   teaspoon (2.25 grams) instant yeast
½   teaspoon onion powder, divided
3   tablespoons (45 grams) water
1   tablespoon (15 grams) whole milk
5   tablespoons (70 grams) unsalted butter, softened and divided
¼   cup (58 grams) butternut squash purée (see Notes)
¾   teaspoon (1 gram) chopped fresh sage
2   (2½- to 2¾-inch-long) fresh sage leaves
Garnish: freshly shredded Parmesan cheese

1. In the bowl of a stand mixer (see Notes) fitted with the paddle attachment, beat ½ cup (63 grams) flour, sugar, ¾ teaspoon (2.25 grams) salt, yeast, and ¼ teaspoon onion powder at low speed until combined.

2. In a small microwave-safe bowl, combine 3 tablespoons (45 grams) water, milk, and 1 tablespoon (14 grams) butter; heat on high in 10-second intervals, stirring between each, until butter is melted and an instant-read thermometer registers 120°F (49°C) to 130°F (54°C). Add warm milk mixture to flour mixture; beat at medium speed for 1 minute, stopping to scrape sides of bowl. Add squash; beat just until combined, about 30 seconds. With mixer on low speed, gradually add ½ cup (63 grams) flour and chopped sage, beating just until combined.

3. Turn out dough onto a very lightly floured surface, and knead by hand until dough passes the windowpane test (see Notes), 10 to 16 minutes; add up to remaining ¼ cup (31 grams) flour, 1 tablespoon (8 grams) at a time, if dough is too wet or sticky. (Dough should be soft and somewhat sticky; re-flour surface only if needed.)

4. Spray a medium bowl with cooking spray. Place dough in bowl, turning to grease top. Cover and let rise in a warm, draft-free place (75°F/24°C) until doubled in size, 40 minutes to 1 hour.

5. In a small saucepan, heat remaining 4 tablespoons (56 grams) butter over medium heat until bubbling. Add sage leaves; cook, stirring occasionally, until leaves are slightly crisp and butter solids are light amber in color and nutty in aroma, 3 to 6 minutes. Transfer butter mixture to a small heatproof bowl; let cool for 15 minutes.

(Butter should be just warm to the touch.) Discard sage leaves. Stir in remaining ¼ teaspoon salt and remaining ¼ teaspoon onion powder.

6. Spray a 4- to 5-cup Bundtlette pan with baking spray with flour.

7. Punch down dough; let stand for 10 minutes. On a clean surface, divide dough into 54 portions (about 4 grams each). Roll each portion into a smooth ball, pinching any seams to seal. (Keep dough portions covered with a sheet of plastic wrap while working.) Dip dough balls in butter mixture, turning until well coated and letting excess drip off; arrange 9 dough balls, side by side, in an even layer in each well. Pour any remaining butter mixture over top of dough, and firmly press balls in an even layer in wells. Cover and let rise in a warm, draft-free place (75°F/24°C) until puffed and dough holds an indentation when pressed, 25 to 35 minutes.

8. Preheat oven to 350°F (180°C).

9. Bake until tops are lightly browned and an instant-read thermometer inserted near center registers 195°F (90°C) to 210°F (98°C), 10 to 14 minutes. Let cool in pan for 5 minutes; invert onto a serving plate. Garnish with cheese, if desired. Serve immediately.

Notes: *We used Diamond Crystal Kosher Salt, which has a different grain shape and a lighter, less salty flavor than coarser kosher salts. If measuring by volume, use half the amount of coarse kosher salt (such as Morton's). Especially for breads, though, it's often safest to measure salt by weight for the most consistent results.*

To make butternut squash purée, halve and seed a medium butternut squash and then coat it on all sides with 1 tablespoon (14 grams) vegetable oil. Bake, cut side down, on a parchment paper-lined baking sheet at 375°F (190°C) until very fork-tender, 50 minutes to 1 hour. Let cool completely on pan. For best color, trim and discard any browned spots. Scoop squash into the work bowl of a food processor, and pulse until mostly smooth, stopping to scrape sides of bowl. (Alternatively, mash using a potato masher.) Reserve any extra squash purée for another use.

We developed this Bundtlette recipe using a 5-quart-capacity stand mixer. If your mixer capacity is too large for this small quantity of dough, you may need to bring this Bundtlette dough together completely by hand.

Test the dough for proper gluten development using the windowpane test. Pinch off (don't tear) a small piece of dough, lightly flouring hands if necessary. Slowly pull the dough out from the center. If the dough is ready, you will be able to stretch it until it's thin and translucent like a windowpane. If the dough tears, it's not quite ready. Knead for 1 minute, and test again.

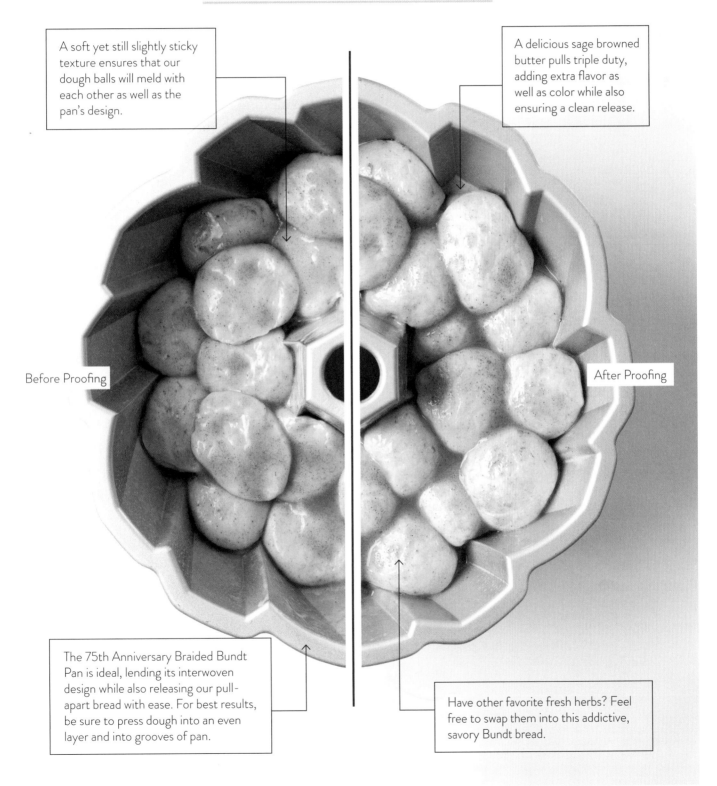

A soft yet still slightly sticky texture ensures that our dough balls will meld with each other as well as the pan's design.

A delicious sage browned butter pulls triple duty, adding extra flavor as well as color while also ensuring a clean release.

Before Proofing

After Proofing

The 75th Anniversary Braided Bundt Pan is ideal, lending its interwoven design while also releasing our pull-apart bread with ease. For best results, be sure to press dough into an even layer and into grooves of pan.

Have other favorite fresh herbs? Feel free to swap them into this addictive, savory Bundt bread.

WALNUT POTICA

Makes 1 (15-cup) loaf

Potica is a traditional celebratory yeasted bread from Slovenia. The soft, rich dough is rolled out and slathered with filling and then rolled up to create a mesmerizing spiral and baked in the shape of a ring or loaf.

1	cup (240 grams) warm whole milk (105°F/41°C to 110°F/43°C)
4½	teaspoons (14 grams) active dry yeast
5¾	cups (719 grams) all-purpose flour
½	cup (100 grams) granulated sugar
2	teaspoons (6 grams) kosher salt
2	large eggs (100 grams), room temperature
1	cup (227 grams) unsalted butter, melted and slightly cooled

Walnut Filling (recipe follows)
Garnish: confectioners' sugar

1. In a small bowl, whisk together warm milk and yeast. Let stand until foamy, about 10 minutes.
2. In the bowl of a stand mixer fitted with the paddle attachment, beat flour, granulated sugar, and salt at low speed until combined. Add eggs. With mixer on low speed, gradually add melted butter. Add yeast mixture, beating until combined, about 30 seconds. Switch to the dough hook attachment. Beat at low speed until dough is smooth and elastic, about 5 minutes. Turn out dough onto a lightly floured surface, and shape into a smooth ball.
3. Spray a large bowl with cooking spray. Place dough in bowl, turning to grease top. Cover and let rise in a warm, draft-free place (75°F/24°C) until doubled in size, about 1 hour.
4. Lightly butter a 15-cup Bundt pan.
5. Punch down dough. On a lightly floured surface, roll dough into a 21x18-inch rectangle. Spread Walnut Filling onto dough, leaving a 1-inch border on one short side. Lightly brush border with water. Starting with short side opposite border, roll dough into a log; press seam to seal. (Be sure to press gently; dough may tear if pinched.) Trim ends. Place log seam side up, and shape into a circle. Brush ends with water, and press together. Using your hands, lift dough, and place in prepared pan. Gently press dough flat. (Don't worry

if dough doesn't look beautiful. It will fill out and bake well once it proofs.) Cover and let rise in a warm, draft-free place (75°F/24°C) until puffed and dough fills three-fourths of pan, 30 to 45 minutes.
6. Preheat oven to 350°F (180°C).
7. Bake until deep golden and an instant-read thermometer inserted near center registers 190°F (88°C), about 50 minutes. Let cool in pan for 15 minutes. Invert potica onto a wire rack, and let cool completely. Garnish with confectioners' sugar, if desired.

WALNUT FILLING

Makes 2½ cups

2	cups (284 grams) walnuts
½	cup (100 grams) granulated sugar
½	cup (170 grams) honey
½	cup (120 grams) whole milk
1	teaspoon (3 grams) kosher salt
1	large egg (50 grams)
1	large egg yolk (19 grams)
1	teaspoon (4 grams) vanilla extract

1. In the work bowl of a food processor, process walnuts until finely ground and uniform in size.
2. In a medium saucepan, stir together sugar, honey, and milk. Cook over medium-low heat, stirring frequently until sugar dissolves and mixture starts to boil. Stir in ground walnuts and salt. Whisk in egg and egg yolk. Cook, whisking constantly, until mixture is slightly thickened and becomes glossy and an instant-read thermometer registers 175°F (79°C) to 180°F (82°C), 6 to 7 minutes.
3. Pour mixture into a medium bowl; stir in vanilla. Cover with a piece of plastic wrap, pressing wrap directly onto surface of filling. Refrigerate until completely cooled. (For a quick cooldown, place bowl in an ice water bath, and let stand, stirring every 5 minutes, until filling cools and thickens.)

PRO TIP
Because of this bread's hefty size and intricate spiral shape, the soft dough may lose its shape easily. If the dough loses its circular shape when transferring to the pan, reposition it as best you can once you've placed it. It doesn't have to be perfect. The dough will rise sumptuously while baking, and you will end up with a beautiful bread.

GARLIC-HERB MONKEY BREAD

Makes 1 (15-cup) Bundt loaf

Looking for something savory to add to your brunch spread? Or maybe a little something extra to accompany dinner? Our finger-friendly pull-apart bread is a scrumptious accompaniment!

3¼ to 3½ cups (406 to 438 grams) all-purpose flour, divided
¼   cup (50 grams) granulated sugar
1   tablespoon (9 grams) plus ¼ teaspoon kosher salt, divided
1   (0.25-ounce) package (7 grams) instant yeast*
¼   teaspoon ground nutmeg
1   cup (240 grams) whole milk
½   cup (113 grams) unsalted butter, softened
1   large egg (50 grams)
½   cup (113 grams) unsalted butter, melted
1½ tablespoons (7 grams) finely chopped fresh chives
1½ tablespoons (6 grams) finely chopped fresh tarragon
1½ tablespoons (6 grams) finely chopped fresh parsley
1   teaspoon (2 grams) garlic powder
¼   teaspoon crushed red pepper
Garnish: freshly grated Parmesan cheese

1. In the bowl of a stand mixer fitted with the paddle attachment, beat 1¼ cups (156 grams) flour, sugar, 1 tablespoon (9 grams) salt, yeast, and nutmeg at low speed until combined.
2. In a medium saucepan, heat milk and softened butter over medium heat until butter is melted and an instant-read thermometer registers 120°F (49°C) to 130°F (54°C). Add warm milk mixture to flour mixture; beat at medium speed for 2 minutes, stopping to scrape sides of bowl. Add egg; beat at medium-high speed for 2 minutes. With mixer on low speed, gradually add 2 cups (250 grams) flour, beating until combined.
3. Switch to the dough hook attachment. Beat at medium-low speed until a soft, somewhat tacky dough forms, 6 to 8 minutes, stopping to scrape sides of bowl and dough hook; add up to

remaining ¼ cup (31 grams) flour, 1 tablespoon (8 grams) at a time, if dough is too sticky. (Dough should pass the windowpane test; see Note.)
4. Spray a large bowl with cooking spray. Place dough in bowl, turning to grease top. Cover and let rise in a warm, draft-free place (75°F/24°C) until doubled in size, 40 minutes to 1 hour.
5. In a small bowl, stir together melted butter, chives, tarragon, parsley, garlic powder, red pepper, and remaining ¼ teaspoon salt.
6. Punch down dough; let stand for 5 minutes. On a clean surface, divide dough into 36 portions (about 24 grams each); gently shape each portion into a ball, pinching closed any seams if needed. (Keep dough portions covered with a sheet of plastic wrap while working.)
7. Spray a 15-cup Bundt pan with baking spray with flour.
8. Dip dough balls in butter mixture, turning until well coated; arrange evenly in prepared pan, pressing dough balls gently into each other and grooves of pan. Cover and let rise in a warm, draft-free place (75°F/24°C) until doubled in size and dough holds an indentation when pressed, 25 to 35 minutes. Reserve remaining butter mixture.
9. Preheat oven to 350°F (180°C).
10. Bake until golden brown and an instant-read thermometer inserted near center registers at least 190°F (88°C), 25 to 30 minutes. Let cool in pan for 5 minutes; invert onto a serving plate.
11. Reheat reserved butter mixture, if necessary; brush onto warm bread. Garnish with cheese, if desired. Serve immediately.

*We used Platinum® Yeast from Red Star®.

Note: *Test the dough for proper gluten development using the windowpane test. Pinch off (don't tear) a small piece of dough. Slowly pull the dough out from the center. If the dough is ready, you will be able to stretch it until it's thin and translucent like a windowpane. If the dough tears, it's not quite ready. Beat for 1 minute, and test again.*

MILK BREAD GIBASSIER

Makes 1 (10-cup) Bundt loaf

This French bake takes on a new look and flavor by combining two of my favorite breads, milk bread and gibassier, and one of my favorite ingredients, orange blossom water.

2¾	cups (349 grams) bread flour
½	cup (100 grams) granulated sugar, divided
1	tablespoon (8 grams) dry milk
2¼	teaspoons (7 grams) instant yeast
2¼	teaspoons (7 grams) kosher salt
½	teaspoon (1 gram) plus ⅛ teaspoon ground cardamom, divided
½	teaspoon ground ginger, divided
½	cup (120 grams) whole milk
	Gibassier Tangzhong (recipe follows)
1	large egg (50 grams), room temperature
1	tablespoon (14 grams) olive oil (not extra-virgin)
1½	teaspoons (7.5 grams) orange blossom water
½	cup (114 grams) unsalted butter, softened and divided
½	cup (80 grams) lightly packed finely chopped candied orange
1½	teaspoons (4.5 grams) anise seeds

1. In the bowl of a stand mixer fitted with the paddle attachment, beat 2 cups (254 grams) flour, ¼ cup (50 grams) sugar, dry milk, yeast, salt, ½ teaspoon (1 gram) cardamom, and ¼ teaspoon ginger at low speed until combined.

2. In a medium saucepan, heat whole milk over medium heat, stirring frequently, until an instant-read thermometer registers 120°F (49°C) to 130°F (54°C). Add warm milk, Gibassier Tangzong, egg, oil, and orange blossom water to flour mixture; beat at medium-low speed until combined, about 1 minute, stopping to scrape sides of bowl. With mixer on low speed, gradually add remaining ¾ cup (95 grams) flour, beating just until combined.

3. Switch to the dough hook attachment. Beat at medium speed until dough begins to pull away from sides of bowl, 10 to 15 minutes, stopping to scrape sides of bowl. (Dough will be extremely sticky to start, but resist the urge to add any flour.) Add ¼ cup (57 grams) butter, 1 tablespoon (14 grams) at a time, beating until completely combined after each addition. Beat until dough is soft and elastic and fully pulls away from sides of bowl, about 10 minutes. Add candied orange and anise seeds, and beat at low speed just until combined. Turn out dough onto a very lightly floured surface; knead 6 to 10 times to help disperse candied orange and anise seeds. Shape dough into a smooth round.

4. Lightly spray a large bowl with cooking spray. Place dough in bowl, turning to grease top. Cover and let rise in a warm, draft-free place (75°F/24°C) until doubled in size, 45 minutes to 1 hour.

5. Punch down dough; cover and let stand for 5 minutes. Spray a 10-cup Bundt pan with baking spray with flour.

6. Turn out dough onto a work surface. Pat or roll dough into an 18x8-inch rectangle, pressing down to completely release all gas from dough and pop any remaining air bubbles. Starting from one long end, roll dough into a tight rope, pressing dough firmly as you roll; pinch seam to seal. Shape dough into a wreath, with seam on inside of wreath. Place dough, seam side up, in prepared pan. Cover and let rise in a warm, draft-free place (75°F/24°C) until dough is puffed and holds an indentation when poked, 30 to 45 minutes.

7. Preheat oven to 350°F (180°C).

8. Bake until golden brown and an instant-read thermometer inserted near center registers at least 195°F (90°C), 25 to 35 minutes. Let cool in pan for 5 minutes. Invert bread onto a wire rack.

9. In a small microwave-safe bowl, heat remaining ¼ cup (57 grams) butter on high in 10-second intervals, stirring between each, until melted.

10. In a small bowl, whisk together remaining ¼ cup (50 grams) sugar, remaining ¼ teaspoon ginger, and remaining ⅛ teaspoon cardamom.

11. Brush melted butter all over warm loaf; sprinkle with sugar mixture. Serve warm, or let cool completely on a wire rack.

GIBASSIER TANGZHONG
Makes about ½ cup

¼	cup (60 grams) whole milk
¼	cup (60 grams) water
3	tablespoons (24 grams) bread flour

1. In a small saucepan, whisk together milk, ¼ cup (60 grams) water, and flour. Cook over medium-low heat, whisking constantly, until thickened and an instant-read thermometer registers 149°F (65°C), 1 to 2 minutes. Transfer to a small bowl, and let cool completely before using.

CAFÉ AU LAIT KUGELHOPF

Makes 1 (10-cup) kugelhopf loaf

With roots in Austria, Germany, France, and Hungary, kugelhopf traditionally includes raisins, but we've given our version a kick of coffee and crunchy nuts.

3½ cups (438 grams) all-purpose flour, divided

⅓ cup (67 grams) plus ¼ cup (50 grams) granulated sugar, divided

½ cup (120 grams) warm whole milk (110°F/43°C to 115°F/46°C)

2¼ teaspoons (7 grams) active dry yeast

1 cup (227 grams) unsalted butter, room temperature

1 teaspoon (3 grams) kosher salt

½ teaspoon (2 grams) vanilla extract

2 large eggs (100 grams), room temperature

⅓ cup (80 grams) warm strong brewed coffee (110°F/43°C to 115°F/46°C)

⅓ cup (38 grams) sliced almonds

Garnish: confectioners' sugar

1. In the bowl of a stand mixer, whisk together ¾ cup (94 grams) flour and ¼ cup (50 grams) granulated sugar by hand.

2. In a small bowl, whisk together warm milk and yeast until yeast dissolves. Add yeast mixture to flour mixture, and whisk until smooth and well combined. Cover and let stand until bubbles form, about 30 minutes.

3. Add butter, salt, vanilla, and remaining ⅓ cup (67 grams) granulated sugar to flour mixture. Using the paddle attachment, beat at medium-low speed until combined. Beat in eggs. With mixer on low speed, add remaining 2¾ cups (344 grams) flour in three additions alternately with warm coffee, beginning and ending with flour, beating just until combined after each addition. Increase mixer speed to medium-high, and beat until smooth, shiny, and elastic and dough pulls completely away from sides of bowl, 9 to 12 minutes. (It is best not to stop mixing during this time).

4. Spray a 10-cup kugelhopf pan or Bundt pan with baking spray with flour. Sprinkle bottom and sides of pan with almonds; using a wooden pick, move almonds around to fill any holes.

5. Using lightly floured hands or a bowl scraper, pinch off small pieces of dough, and place in prepared pan. Using lightly floured fingers, press dough even and flat. Gently tap pan on a kitchen towel-lined counter a few times. Cover and let rise in a warm, draft-free place (75°F/24°C) until dough is about 1½ inches from top of pan, 1½ to 2 hours.

6. Preheat oven to 350°F (180°C).

7. Bake until golden and an instant-read thermometer inserted near center registers 190°F (88°C), 30 to 35 minutes. Let cool in pan for 10 minutes. Invert kugelhopf onto a wire rack, and let cool completely. Garnish with confectioners' sugar, if desired.

EVERYTHING BAGEL BUNDTWICH BREAD

Makes 1 (10-cup) Bundt loaf

We've taken a favorite savory morning bread and turned it into the best sandwich bread. Serve it at your next picnic or potluck for a guaranteed crowd pleaser.

3¼ to 3½ cups (406 to 437 grams) all-purpose flour, divided
¼ cup (50 grams) granulated sugar
2½ teaspoons (7.5 grams) kosher salt
2¼ teaspoons (7 grams) instant yeast
½ teaspoon (1 gram) garlic powder*
1 cup (240 grams) whole milk
½ cup (113 grams) unsalted butter, softened
1 large egg (50 grams), room temperature
½ cup (56 grams) finely chopped green onion
1 teaspoon (3 grams) poppy seeds*
1 teaspoon (3 grams) assorted sesame seeds*
1 teaspoon (2 grams) dried minced onion
1 tablespoon (14 grams) unsalted butter, melted
Garnish: poppy seeds, assorted sesame seeds, dried minced onion, flaked sea salt

1. In the bowl of a stand mixer fitted with the paddle attachment, beat 1¼ cups (156 grams) flour, sugar, kosher salt, yeast, and garlic powder at low speed until combined.

2. In a medium saucepan, heat milk and softened butter over medium heat until butter is melted and an instant-read thermometer registers 120°F (49°C) to 130°F (54°C). Add warm milk mixture to flour mixture; beat at medium speed for 2 minutes, stopping to scrape sides of bowl. Add egg; beat at medium-high speed for 2 minutes. With mixer on low speed, gradually add 2 cups (250 grams) flour, green onion, poppy seeds, sesame seeds, and dried onion, beating until combined.

3. Switch to the dough hook attachment. Beat at low speed until a soft, shiny, somewhat tacky dough forms, 8 to 12 minutes, stopping to scrape sides of bowl and dough hook; add up to remaining ¼ cup (31 grams) flour, 1 tablespoon (8 grams) at a time, if dough is too sticky. (Dough will clear sides of bowl and should pass the windowpane test; see Note.)

4. Spray a large bowl with cooking spray. Place dough in bowl, turning to grease top. Cover and let rise in a warm, draft-free place (75°F/24°C) until doubled in size, 40 minutes to 1 hour.

5. Punch down dough, and let stand for 10 minutes.

6. Spray a 10-cup Bundt pan with baking spray with flour.

7. Divide dough in half. On a clean surface, press and shape half of dough into a rough 9½x4-inch rectangle. Starting on one long side, press and fold dough, about ½ inch at a time, pressing to seal each time before folding again. Repeat to create about a 12-inch rope; pinch seam to seal. (Dough rope will naturally lengthen as it's rolled.) Place dough roll, seam side facing toward pan's inner tube, in prepared pan, pressing and scrunching roll in on itself to fit in half of pan. Repeat with remaining dough, scrunching dough ropes so they are placed end to end; press both halves into an even layer in pan. Cover and let rise in a warm, draft-free place (75°F/24°C) until dough is puffed and holds an indentation when poked, 25 to 35 minutes.

8. Preheat oven to 350°F (180°C).

9. Bake until golden brown and an instant-read thermometer inserted near center registers at least 195°F (90°C) to 200°F (93°C), 22 to 28 minutes, loosely covering with foil after 20 minutes of baking to prevent excess browning if necessary. Let cool in pan for 5 minutes. Invert bread onto a wire rack. Brush melted butter all over bread. Garnish top with poppy seeds, sesame seeds, dried onion, and sea salt, if desired. Serve warm, or let cool completely.

We used Simply Organic Garlic Powder, Simply Organic Poppy Seed, Simply Organic Black Sesame Seed, and Simply Organic Sesame Seed.

Note: *Test the dough for proper gluten development using the windowpane test. Lightly flour hands and pinch off (don't tear) a small piece of dough. Slowly pull the dough out from the center. If the dough is ready, you will be able to stretch it until it's thin and translucent like a windowpane. If the dough tears, it's not quite ready. Beat for 1 minute, and test again.*

HONEY & RYE'S MONKEY BREAD

Makes 1 (12-cup) Bundt loaf

Recipe courtesy of Anne Andrus, Honey & Rye Bakehouse

A signature sweet at Honey & Rye Bakehouse in Minneapolis, Minnesota, this monkey bread is everything you want in a cozy cold-weather bake: soft, pillowy dough spiced with warm cinnamon and covered in a caramel-like syrup.

4⅔	cups (583 grams) all-purpose flour
1¾	cups (350 grams) granulated sugar, divided
4½	teaspoons (14 grams) instant yeast
4	teaspoons (12 grams) kosher salt
½	cup (120 grams) hot water (120°F/49°C to 130°F/54°C)
½	cup (120 grams) hot whole milk (120°F/49°C to 130°F/54°C)
3	large eggs (150 grams), room temperature
1½	teaspoons (6 grams) vanilla extract
¾	cup plus 2 tablespoons (196 grams) unsalted butter, cubed and room temperature
4	teaspoons (10 grams) ground cinnamon

Monkey Goo (recipe follows)

1. In the bowl of a stand mixer, whisk together flour, ¼ cup (50 grams) sugar, yeast, and salt by hand. Add ½ cup (120 grams) hot water, hot milk, eggs, and vanilla. Using the paddle attachment, beat at low speed until a shaggy dough forms.
2. Switch to the dough hook attachment. Beat at low speed until a tight, elastic dough forms, about 12 minutes. Add butter, a few cubes at a time, and beat until butter is incorporated and dough is smooth, elastic, and glossy, 45 to 50 minutes. (This very enriched dough takes more time to mix than average; slow and steady mixing ensures your mixer won't overheat.) Turn out dough onto a lightly floured surface, and shape into a smooth round.
3. Lightly oil a large bowl. Place dough in bowl, turning to grease top. Cover and let rise in a warm, draft-free place (75°F/24°C) until doubled in size, 25 to 30 minutes.
4. In a medium bowl, stir together cinnamon and remaining 1½ cups (300 grams) sugar.

5. Punch down dough, and let stand for 10 minutes. Turn out dough onto a very lightly floured surface, and divide in half. Roll half of dough into a 1-inch-thick rope. (Keep remaining dough covered to prevent it from drying out.) Cut dough rope into 1-inch pieces, and place in cinnamon sugar, tossing to coat. Set aside, and repeat with remaining dough.
6. Spray a 12-cup Bundt pan with baking spray with flour. Pour half of Monkey Goo (about ¾ cup or 227 grams) into bottom of prepared pan. Fill pan with cinnamon sugar-covered dough pieces. (Pan will be three-fourths full.) Pour remaining Monkey Goo on top. Cover and refrigerate overnight.
7. Let stand at room temperature for 45 minutes to 1 hour.
8. Preheat oven to 350°F (180°C).
9. Loosely cover pan with foil.
10. Bake for 30 minutes. Uncover and bake until top is deep golden brown and an instant-read thermometer inserted near center registers 190°F (88°C), 20 to 25 minutes more. Let cool in pan on a wire rack for 10 minutes. Invert loaf onto a rimmed serving plate. Serve warm.

MONKEY GOO
Makes 1¾ cups

1	cup (220 grams) firmly packed light brown sugar
½	cup (113 grams) unsalted butter
3	tablespoons (63 grams) honey
3½	tablespoons (52 grams) heavy whipping cream, room temperature
3½	tablespoons (52 grams) water, room temperature
½	teaspoon (1.5 grams) kosher salt

1. In a medium saucepan, heat brown sugar, butter, and honey over medium heat, whisking occasionally, until sugar dissolves and mixture is combined. Bring to a boil; cook until foamy and a thick syrup forms, 5 to 8 minutes. Remove from heat, and whisk in cream, 3½ tablespoons (52 grams) water, and salt. Let cool completely before using.

Photo by Chelsie Lopez

JALAPEÑO-CHEDDAR MONKEY BREAD

Makes 1 (15-cup) Bundt loaf

This tear-and-share treat is so munchable that you might just eat it as a snack supper—don't say we didn't warn you.

3¼ to 3½ cups (406 to 438 grams) all-purpose flour, divided
1½ cups (171 grams) freshly shredded sharp white Cheddar cheese, divided
¼ cup (50 grams) granulated sugar
1 tablespoon (9 grams) plus ¼ teaspoon kosher salt, divided
2¼ teaspoons (7 grams) instant yeast
1 cup (240 grams) whole milk
½ cup (113 grams) unsalted butter, softened
1 large egg (50 grams)
½ cup (113 grams) unsalted butter, melted
¼ cup (40 grams) minced seeded jalapeños
1 tablespoon (4 grams) chopped fresh thyme
1 tablespoon (3 grams) chopped fresh oregano
1 teaspoon (3 grams) granulated garlic
1 teaspoon (3 grams) granulated onion

1. In the bowl of a stand mixer fitted with the paddle attachment, beat 1¼ cups (156 grams) flour, ½ cup (57 grams) cheese, sugar, 1 tablespoon (9 grams) salt, and yeast at low speed until combined.
2. In a medium saucepan, heat milk and softened butter over medium heat until butter is melted and an instant-read thermometer registers 120°F (49°C) to 130°F (54°C). Add warm milk mixture to flour mixture; beat at medium speed for 2 minutes, stopping to scrape sides of bowl. Add egg; beat at medium-high speed for 2 minutes. With mixer on low speed, gradually add 2 cups (250 grams) flour, beating until combined.
3. Switch to the dough hook attachment. Beat at medium-low speed until a soft, somewhat tacky dough forms, 12 to 14 minutes, stopping to scrape sides of bowl and dough hook; add up to remaining ¼ cup (31 grams) flour, 1 tablespoon (8 grams) at a time, if dough is too sticky. (Dough should pass the windowpane test; see Note.) Shape dough into a smooth round.

4. Spray a large bowl with cooking spray. Place dough in bowl, turning to grease top. Cover and let rise in a warm, draft-free place (75°F/24°C) until doubled in size, 40 minutes to 1 hour.
5. In a small bowl, stir together melted butter, jalapeños, thyme, oregano, granulated garlic, granulated onion, and remaining ¼ teaspoon salt. In a small bowl, place remaining 1 cup cheese (114 grams).
6. Punch down dough; let stand for 5 minutes. On a clean surface, divide dough into 36 portions (about 27 grams each); gently shape each portion into a ball, pinching closed any seams if needed. (Keep dough portions covered with a sheet of plastic wrap to prevent a skin from forming.)
7. Spray a 15-cup Bundt pan with baking spray with flour.
8. Dip dough balls in butter mixture, turning until well coated, and shaking off excess. Dip dough balls in cheese to lightly adhere. Arrange dough balls evenly in prepared pan, gently pressing into each other and grooves of pan. Cover and let rise in a warm, draft-free place (75°F/24°C) until doubled in size and dough holds an indentation when pressed, 25 to 35 minutes. Drizzle any remaining butter mixture onto dough.
9. Preheat oven to 350°F (180°C).
10. Bake until golden brown and an instant-read thermometer inserted near center registers at least 190°F (88°C), 25 to 30 minutes. Let cool in pan for 5 minutes; invert onto a serving plate. Serve warm.

Note: *To use the windowpane test to check dough for proper gluten development, lightly flour hands and pinch off (don't tear) a small piece of dough. Slowly pull the dough out from the center. If the dough is ready, you will be able to stretch it until it's thin and translucent like a windowpane. If the dough tears, it's not quite ready. Beat for 1 minute, and test again.*

CINNAMON ROLL BUNDT

Makes 1 (10-cup) Bundt loaf

An ode to the morning classic, this hypnotizingly swirled Bundt takes soft and sticky cinnamon rolls to the next level. Showing off the exciting versatility of the Bundt pan, we swapped out traditional cake batter for layers of yeast-leavened sweet dough in this stunning changeup.

3¼ to 3½ cups (406 to 437 grams) all-purpose flour, divided
¼ cup (50 grams) granulated sugar
2¼ teaspoons (7 grams) instant yeast
2⅛ teaspoons (6 grams) kosher salt, divided
1 cup (240 grams) whole milk
½ cup (113 grams) unsalted butter, softened
1 large egg (50 grams), room temperature
⅔ cup (147 grams) firmly packed light brown sugar
4 teaspoons (8 grams) ground cinnamon
¼ teaspoon ground nutmeg
4 tablespoons (56 grams) unsalted butter, melted and divided
Cream Cheese Glaze (recipe follows)

1. In the bowl of a stand mixer fitted with the paddle attachment, beat 1¼ cups (156 grams) flour, granulated sugar, yeast, and 2 teaspoons (6 grams) salt at low speed until combined.
2. In a medium saucepan, heat milk and softened butter over medium heat until butter is melted and an instant-read thermometer registers 120°F (49°C) to 130°F (54°C). Add warm milk mixture to flour mixture; beat at medium speed for 2 minutes, stopping to scrape sides of bowl. Add egg; beat at medium-high speed for 2 minutes. With mixer on low speed, gradually add 2 cups (250 grams) flour, beating until combined.
3. Switch to the dough hook attachment. Beat at medium-low speed until a soft, somewhat tacky dough forms, 6 to 8 minutes, stopping to scrape sides of bowl and dough hook. Add up to remaining ¼ cup (31 grams) flour, 1 tablespoon (8 grams) at a time as needed if dough is too sticky. (Dough should pass the windowpane test; see Note.)
4. Spray a large bowl with cooking spray. Place dough in bowl, turning to grease top. Cover and let rise in a warm, draft-free place (75°F/24°C) until doubled in size, 40 to 50 minutes.

5. In a small bowl, stir together brown sugar, cinnamon, nutmeg, and remaining ⅛ teaspoon salt until well combined.
6. Lightly punch down dough. Cover and let stand for 10 minutes. Turn out dough onto a clean surface, and roll into a 26x7-inch rectangle. Brush 2 tablespoons (28 grams) melted butter onto dough, leaving a ½-inch border on one long side. Sprinkle brown sugar mixture onto butter. (It will be a generous brown sugar layer.) Starting with long side opposite border, roll up dough, jelly roll style; pinch seam to seal. Place seam side down, and gently shape to 26 inches long and even thickness, if necessary. Using a serrated knife, cut log into 26 slices (about 1 inch thick each); dip knife in flour as needed.
7. Spray a 10-cup Bundt pan with baking spray with flour. Arrange slices evenly in prepared pan as desired, placing some slices with cut sides facing out around edges of pan and recoiling any slices tighter as necessary; press slices firmly into each other and grooves of pan. Cover and let rise in a warm, draft-free place (75°F/24°C) until puffed and dough holds an indentation when pressed, 25 to 35 minutes.
8. Preheat oven to 350°F (180°C).
9. Bake until golden brown and an instant-read thermometer inserted near center registers at least 190°F (88°C), 25 to 30 minutes. Let cool in pan for 5 minutes. Invert loaf onto a serving plate. Brush with remaining 2 tablespoons (28 grams) melted butter. Serve warm or at room temperature with Cream Cheese Glaze.

Note: *Test the dough for proper gluten development using the windowpane test. Pinch off (don't tear) a small piece of dough, lightly flouring hands if necessary. Slowly pull the dough out from the center. If the dough is ready, you will be able to stretch it until it's thin and translucent like a windowpane. If the dough tears, it's not quite ready. Beat for 1 minute, and test again.*

CREAM CHEESE GLAZE

Makes about 1½ cups

3 ounces (85 grams) cream cheese, softened
1 cup (120 grams) confectioners' sugar
1 tablespoon (15 grams) whole milk
1 tablespoon (14 grams) unsalted butter, melted

1. In the bowl of a stand mixer fitted with the paddle attachment, beat cream cheese at medium speed until smooth. With mixer on low speed, gradually add confectioners' sugar, beating until combined. Add milk and melted butter; beat until smooth and well combined. Use immediately.

bake it a BUNDTLETTE

CINNAMON ROLL BUNDTLETTES

Makes 4 Bundtlettes

1 to 1¼ cups (126 to 157 grams) all-purpose flour, divided
1½   tablespoons (18 grams) granulated sugar
¾   teaspoon (2.25 grams) kosher salt
¾   teaspoon (2.25 grams) instant yeast
⅓   cup (80 grams) whole milk
3   tablespoons (42 grams) unsalted butter, softened
1   large egg yolk (19 grams), room temperature
¼   cup (55 grams) firmly packed light brown sugar
¾   teaspoon (1.5 grams) ground cinnamon
Pinch ground nutmeg (optional)
2   tablespoons (28 grams) unsalted butter, melted and divided
Cream Cheese Glaze for Bundtlettes (recipe follows)

1. In the bowl of a stand mixer fitted with the paddle attachment, beat ½ cup (63 grams) flour, granulated sugar, salt, and yeast at low speed until combined.

2. In a small saucepan, heat milk and softened butter over medium heat, stirring occasionally, until butter is melted and an instant-read thermometer registers 120°F (49°C) to 130°F (54°C). Add warm milk mixture to flour mixture; beat at medium speed for 2 minutes, stopping to scrape sides of bowl. Add egg yolk; beat at medium-high speed for 2 minutes. With mixer on low speed, gradually add ½ cup (63 grams) flour, beating until combined.

3. Switch to the dough hook attachment. Beat at medium-low speed until a soft, somewhat tacky dough forms, about 6 minutes, stopping to scrape sides of bowl and dough hook. Add up to remaining ¼ cup (31 grams) flour, 1 tablespoon (8 grams) at a time as needed if dough is too sticky. Turn out dough onto a clean surface, and knead by hand until dough passes windowpane test (see Notes.)

4. Spray a medium bowl with cooking spray. Place dough in bowl, turning to grease top. Cover and let rise in a warm, draft-free place (75°F/24°C) until doubled in size, 1 to 1½ hours.

5. In a small bowl, stir together brown sugar, cinnamon, and nutmeg (if using) until well combined.

6. Lightly punch down dough. Cover and let stand for 10 minutes. Turn out dough onto a clean surface, and roll into a 22x3½-inch rectangle. Brush 1 tablespoon (14 grams) melted butter onto dough, leaving a ½-inch border on one long side. Sprinkle brown sugar mixture evenly onto butter. (It will be a generous layer.) Starting with long side opposite border, roll up dough, jelly roll style; pinch seam to seal. Place log seam side down, and gently shape to 22 inches long and even thickness, if necessary. Using a serrated knife dipped in flour, cut log into 42 slices (about ¼ to ½ inch thick each).

7. Spray 4 wells of a 4- or 5-cup Bundtlette pan (see Notes) with baking spray with flour. Divide and arrange slices in prepared wells as desired, pressing slices firmly into each other and grooves of pan. Cover and let rise in a warm, draft-free place (75°F/24°C) until puffed and dough holds an indentation when pressed, 40 minutes to 1 hour.

8. Preheat oven to 350°F (180°C).

9. Bake until golden brown and an instant-read thermometer inserted near center registers at least 190°F (88°C), 8 to 10 minutes. Let cool in pan for 5 minutes. Invert loaves onto a wire rack. Brush with remaining 1 tablespoon (14 grams) melted butter. Serve warm or at room temperature with Cream Cheese Glaze.

Notes: *Test the dough for proper gluten development using the windowpane test. Pinch off (don't tear) a small piece of dough, lightly flouring hands if necessary. Slowly pull the dough out from the center. If the dough is ready, you will be able to stretch it until it's thin and translucent like a windowpane. If the dough tears, it's not quite ready. Knead for 1 minute, and test again.*

This recipe bakes best in a pan with a simple, rounded, scalloped design like the Nordic Ware Anniversary Bundtlette Pan.

CREAM CHEESE GLAZE FOR BUNDTLETTES
Makes ½ cup

2   ounces (57 grams) cream cheese, softened
⅔   cup (80 grams) confectioners' sugar
2   teaspoons (10 grams) whole milk
2   teaspoons (10 grams) unsalted butter, melted

1. In a medium bowl, stir cream cheese until smooth and creamy. Gradually add confectioners' sugar, stirring until combined. Add milk and melted butter; whisk until smooth and well combined. Use immediately.

The Elegant Party Bundt Pan's rounded, scalloped design is ideal to show off the cinnamon rolls' mesmerizing swirls, which would otherwise get lost in a more intricate pan.

The glaze will be thinner if applied to a warm Bundt. If serving warm, you may want to serve the glaze on the side and drizzle it onto individual slices.

A 5-minute cooling time is the sweet spot to ensure this Bundt's release and avoid any sugar-induced sticking.

A soft, enriched dough perfectly melds into the pan's grooves and releases with ease. Be sure to press slices firmly together and into crevices before the final proof.

For swirled success, arrange the slices so the spiraled designs are visible along the bottom and sides of the pan, overlapping the rolls slightly. Then layer in the remaining slices as desired to create a level dough ring.

POLISH BABKA

Makes 1 (15-cup) Bundt loaf

Our babka is studded with golden raisins, candied oranges, and dried cranberries and is served with a special glaze that makes it fit for any celebration.

3¾   cups (469 grams) all-purpose flour, divided
⅓   cup (67 grams) granulated sugar
3½   teaspoons (10.5 grams) instant yeast
2   teaspoons (6 grams) kosher salt
1   cup (240 grams) whole milk
¾   cup (170 grams) unsalted butter, cubed and softened
5   large eggs (250 grams), room temperature
1   tablespoon (10 grams) tightly packed orange zest
2   teaspoons (12 grams) vanilla bean paste
⅓   cup (56 grams) lightly packed chopped golden raisins
⅓   cup (55 grams) lightly packed ¼-inch-chopped candied oranges
⅓   cup (52 grams) lightly packed chopped dried sweetened cranberries
Sparkling Wine Syrup (recipe follows)
Confectioners' sugar, for dusting
Sparkling Wine Glaze (recipe follows)

1. In the bowl of a stand mixer fitted with the paddle attachment, beat 1 cup (125 grams) flour, sugar, yeast, and salt at low speed just until combined.
2. In a medium saucepan, heat milk and butter over medium heat, stirring occasionally, until butter is melted and an instant-read thermometer registers 120°F (49°C) to 130°F (54°C). Add warm milk mixture to flour mixture; beat at medium-low speed for 2 minutes, stopping to scrape sides of bowl. Add eggs, orange zest, vanilla bean paste, and remaining 2¾ cups (344 grams) flour; beat at low speed just until combined. Increase mixer speed to high, and beat for 2 minutes, stopping to scrape sides of bowl. (Mixture consistency will be a cross between a thick cake batter and a very wet dough.) Fold in raisins, candied oranges, and cranberries just until combined. Cover with a sheet of greased plastic wrap, and let rise in a warm, draft-free place (75°F/24°C) until doubled in size, about 1 hour.
3. Spray a 15-cup Bundt pan with baking spray with flour.
4. Stir down batter, releasing as many air bubbles as possible; spoon batter into prepared pan. Tap pan on a kitchen towel–lined counter several times to settle batter and release any air bubbles. Cover with a sheet of greased plastic wrap, and let rise in a warm, draft-free place (75°F/24°C) until doubled in size, about 30 minutes. (Pan will look quite full but will not overflow while baking.)
5. Preheat oven to 350°F (180°C).
6. Bake until golden and an instant-read thermometer inserted near center registers 190°F (88°C), 25 to 35 minutes, rotating pan halfway through baking and loosely covering with foil to prevent excess browning, if necessary. Let cool in pan for 10 minutes. Using a small offset spatula or a butter knife, loosen babka from center of pan; invert onto a wire rack.
7. Pour half of Sparkling Wine Syrup into pan, and carefully return babka to pan. Pour remaining Sparkling Wine Syrup all over babka; let stand for 5 minutes. Invert babka onto a lightly greased wire rack placed on a rimmed baking sheet; let cool completely. Dust with confectioners' sugar, and serve with Sparkling Wine Glaze.

SPARKLING WINE SYRUP
Makes about 2¼ cups

1¼   cups (250 grams) granulated sugar
1⅔   cups (378 grams) dry sparkling white wine

1. In a small saucepan, cook sugar and ⅔ cup (152 grams) wine over medium-high heat, stirring frequently, until sugar dissolves and mixture comes to a boil. Remove from heat; transfer sugar mixture to a small bowl. Stir in remaining 1 cup (226 grams) wine. Let cool.

SPARKLING WINE GLAZE
Makes about 1 cup

2½   cups (300 grams) confectioners' sugar
¼   cup (56 grams) dry sparkling white wine
½   teaspoon (1.5 grams) kosher salt

1. In a medium bowl, whisk together all ingredients until smooth and well combined. Use immediately.

BABÀ RUSTICO

Makes 1 (10-cup) Bundt loaf

The French may have charcuterie, but in this Babà Rustico recipe, Italian antipasto reigns supreme. A classic of Neapolitan cuisine, the Babà Rustico is a savory yeasted bread often baked in a ring mold with an array of savory fillings. Simultaneously salty, savory, and rich, this beautiful bread is dinner party-ready but also amazing served sliced and toasted alongside eggs at breakfast. It's truly a bread fit for any occasion.

2½   cups (318 grams) bread flour, divided
½   cup (48 grams) freshly grated Parmesan cheese
3   tablespoons (12 grams) chopped fresh parsley
2   teaspoons (6 grams) kosher salt
¼   teaspoon ground black pepper
1   cup (240 grams) warm whole milk (110°F/43°C to 115°F/46°C)
1   (0.25-ounce) package (7 grams) instant yeast*
1   teaspoon (4 grams) granulated sugar
4½   tablespoons (63 grams) neutral oil
2   large eggs (100 grams), room temperature
¾   cup (130 grams) ⅜-inch-cubed sharp provolone cheese
½   cup (80 grams) chopped salami Napoli
½   cup (90 grams) chopped prosciutto cotto
Garnish: chopped fresh parsley

1. In a medium bowl, whisk together 1½ cups (191 grams) flour, Parmesan, parsley, salt, and pepper.

2. In the bowl of a stand mixer, whisk together warm milk, yeast, and sugar by hand. Let stand until foamy, about 5 minutes. Add remaining 1 cup (127 grams) flour; using the paddle attachment, beat at low speed until smooth and well combined, about 1 minute. Add oil and eggs, and beat until well combined. With mixer on low speed, gradually add flour mixture, beating until well combined and stopping to scrape sides of bowl. Increase mixer speed to medium-high, and beat until dough is smooth, shiny, and elastic, 8 to 10 minutes. (Dough will still stick to sides and bottom of bowl.) Reduce mixer speed to low, and gradually add provolone, salami, and prosciutto cotto until combined. (If you do not feel like the mix-ins are well distributed by the mixer, you can dip your hand in water, as needed, and fold and squeeze the dough to help distribute the mix-ins more evenly.) Cover and let stand at room temperature for 10 minutes.

3. Spray a 10-cup Bundt pan with baking spray with flour. Using a bowl scraper or spatula, spoon dough in small amounts evenly into prepared pan. Using wet fingers, press dough into pan, even and flat. Tap pan on a kitchen towel-lined counter a few times. Cover and let rise in a warm, draft-free place (75°F/24°C) until dough is puffed and about 1 inch from top of pan, 30 to 45 minutes.

4. Preheat oven to 350°F (180°C).

5. Bake until golden and an instant-read thermometer inserted in center registers 190°F (88°C) to 200°F (93°C), 25 to 30 minutes. Let cool in pan for 5 minutes. Invert bread onto a wire rack, and let cool for at least 15 minutes. Garnish with parsley, if desired. Serve warm. Refrigerate in an airtight container for up to 2 days.

We used Platinum® Yeast from Red Star®.

MAPLE-WALNUT MONKEY MILK BREAD

Makes 1 (10-cup) Bundt loaf

Warmed with our Chinese Five-Spice Mix and sweetened with golden maple syrup, this nutty pull-apart dream will disappear in a flash.

3¼ to 3½ cups (406 to 437 grams) all-purpose flour
1¾ cups (350 grams) plus ⅓ cup (67 grams) granulated sugar, divided
2½ teaspoons (7.5 grams) kosher salt
2¼ teaspoons (7 grams) instant yeast
⅔ cup (160 grams) whole milk
½ cup (113 grams) unsalted butter, divided
1 tablespoon (14 grams) neutral oil
Tangzhong (recipe follows)
1 large egg (50 grams), room temperature
1 teaspoon (2 grams) Chinese Five-Spice Mix (recipe follows)
½ cup (113 grams) unsalted butter, melted
1 cup (113 grams) roughly chopped walnuts
½ cup (170 grams) maple syrup

1. In the bowl of a stand mixer fitted with the paddle attachment, beat 1 cup (125 grams) flour, ⅓ cup (67 grams) sugar, salt, and yeast at low speed until combined.
2. In a medium saucepan, heat milk, ¼ cup (57 grams) butter, and oil over medium heat, stirring frequently, until butter is melted and an instant-read thermometer registers 120°F (49°C) to 130°F (54°C). Add warm milk mixture and Tangzhong to flour mixture; beat at low speed until well combined. Add egg, and beat until well combined. With mixer on low speed, gradually add 2¼ cups (281 grams) flour, beating just until combined.
3. Switch to the dough hook attachment. Beat at low speed until a soft, tacky dough forms, 12 to 14 minutes, stopping to scrape sides of bowl; add up to remaining ¼ cup (31 grams) flour, 1 tablespoon (8 grams) at a time, if dough is too sticky.
4. Lightly spray a large bowl with cooking spray. Place dough in bowl, turning to grease top. Cover and let rise in a warm, draft-free place (75°F/24°C) until doubled in size, 40 minutes to 1 hour.
5. Spray a 10-cup Bundt pan with baking spray with flour.
6. In a small bowl, stir together 1 cup (200 grams) sugar and Chinese Five-Spice Mix. In another small bowl, place melted butter.
7. Punch down dough; cover and let stand for 5 minutes. Turn out dough onto a clean surface, and divide in half (about 430 grams each). Roll each half into a 24-inch rope. Cut each rope into 1-inch pieces (24 pieces for each rope; about 18 grams each). Working in batches, dip dough pieces in melted butter; toss in sugar mixture to coat, shaking off excess.
8. In bottom of prepared pan, place ⅓ cup (38 grams) walnuts. Arrange a layer of dough in bottom of pan. Sprinkle ⅓ cup (38 grams) walnuts on top of dough in pan, and arrange a layer of

dough on top. Repeat with remaining ⅓ cup (38 grams) walnuts and remaining dough. Cover and let rise in a warm, draft-free place (75°F/24°C) until puffed and dough fills pan, 20 to 30 minutes.
9. Preheat oven to 350°F (180°C).
10. In a small saucepan, melt remaining ¼ cup (57 grams) butter over medium-high heat. Stir in maple syrup and remaining ¾ cup (150 grams) sugar. Bring to a boil; cook until sugar is melted, 3 to 4 minutes. Pour onto dough in pan.
11. Bake until golden brown and an instant-read thermometer inserted in center registers at least 190°F (88°C), 50 to 55 minutes, covering with foil after 35 minutes of baking to prevent excess browning. Let cool in pan for 15 minutes. Invert loaf onto a serving plate; serve warm. Best served same day.

TANGZHONG
Makes about ⅓ cup

⅓ cup (80 grams) whole milk
2 tablespoons (16 grams) all-purpose flour

1. In a small saucepan, whisk together milk and flour. Cook over medium-low heat, whisking constantly, until mixture is thickened, whisk leaves lines on bottom of pan, and an instant-read thermometer registers 150°F (66°C). Transfer to a small bowl, and let cool before using (no hotter than 130°F/57°C) or to room temperature.

CHINESE FIVE-SPICE MIX
Makes about ½ cup

2 tablespoons (14 grams) whole fennel seed
5 whole star anise (5 grams)
2 teaspoons (4 grams) whole Szechuan peppercorns
1 teaspoon (3 grams) whole cloves
2 tablespoons (12 grams) ground cinnamon

1. In a small skillet, cook fennel seed, star anise, peppercorns, and cloves over low heat, stirring frequently, until fragrant, 8 to 10 minutes. Place in a spice grinder; grind until a fine powder. Sift into a small bowl; stir in cinnamon. Store in an airtight container for up to 1 year.

recipe index

credits

Editor-in-Chief Brian Hart Hoffman
VP/Culinary & Custom Content
Brooke Michael Bell
Editorial Director Nancy Meeks
Art Director Liz Kight
Associate Editor Amber Wilson
Assistant Editor Chessa Parker
Senior Copy Editor Meg Lundberg
Editorial Assistant Christina Fleisch
Senior Digital Imaging Specialist
Delisa McDaniel

Test Kitchen Director Laura Crandall
Food Stylists/Recipe Developers
Aaron Conrad, Katie Moon Dickerson,
Amanda Stabile
Contributing Recipe Developer
Nancy McHughes

Senior Stylist Sidney Bragiel
Stylists Maghan Armstrong, Courtni Bodiford,
Lucy Finney, Maggie Hill, Mary Beth Jones

Senior Photographer Mac Jamieson
Photographers Jim Bathie, Kyle Carpenter,
John O'Hagan, Stephanie Welbourne Steele

Cover
Photography by Kyle Carpenter
Recipe Development by Amanda Stabile
Food Styling by Katie Moon Dickerson
Styling by Maggie Hill